Reading and Note Taking Study Guide

UNITED STATES HISTORY

PEARSON

Boston, Massachusetts • Chandler, Arizona • Glenview, Illinois • New York, New York

Acknowledgments
Grateful acknowledgment is made to the following for copyrighted material:

Images:
Cover: Juanmonino/Getty Images

Copyright © Pearson Education, Inc., or its affiliates. All rights reserved. Printed in the United States of America. This publication is protected by copyright, and permission should be obtained from the publisher prior to any prohibited reproduction, storage in a retrieval system, or transmission in any form or by any means, electronic, mechanical, photocopying, recording, or otherwise. For information regarding permissions, request forms and the appropriate contacts within the Pearson Education Global Rights & Permissions department, please visit www.pearsoned.com/permissions.

PEARSON is an exclusive trademark owned by Pearson Education, Inc., or its affiliates in the U.S. and/or other countries.

ISBN-13: 978-0-32-888033-1

ISBN-10:   0-32-888033-7

Contents

United States History
Reading and Note Taking Study Guide

How to Use the Reading and Note Taking Study Guide v

Topic 1
America's Cultural Roots
Note Taking Study Guide. 1
Lesson 1: The Peoples of the Americas 2
Lesson 2: The West Africans. 3
Lesson 3: Europeans Make Contact 4
Lesson 4: Spain and France in the Americas. 6
Review Questions 9

Topic 2
England's American Colonies
Note Taking Study Guide. 11
Lesson 1: The Southern Colonies Take Root 12
Lesson 2: New Lives in New England 13
Lesson 3: The Middle Colonies Thrive. 14
Lesson 4: Immigration and Slavery in the Colonies. 15
Lesson 5: Economic and Social Life in the Colonies. 16
Lesson 6: Creating an American Identity. . . 18
Review Questions 19

Topic 3
The American Revolution
Note Taking Study Guide. 21
Lesson 1: The French and Indian War 22
Lesson 2: Causes of the Revolution 23
Lesson 3: The Colonists Declare Independence. 24
Lesson 4: Americans Win the Revolution . . 25
Review Questions 27

Topic 4
Establishing the New Nation
Note Taking Study Guide. 28
Lesson 1: The Articles of Confederation . . . 29
Lesson 2: The Constitutional Convention . . 30
Lesson 3: The Enduring Constitution. 31
Review Questions 33

Topic 5
The Early Republic
Note Taking Study Guide. 34
Lesson 1: The New Government Finds Its Way 35
Lesson 2: Jefferson as President. 37
Lesson 3: The War of 1812 38
Lesson 4: The Beginning of the Industrial Revolution 39
Lesson 5: Differences Between North and South Grow 40
Lesson 6: Nationalism Influences Policies. . 41
Lesson 7: Jacksonian Democracy. 42
Review Questions 44

Topic 6
Reshaping America in the Early 1800s
Note Taking Study Guide. 46
Lesson 1: Moving West. 47
Lesson 2: Texas and the Mexican-American War 48
Lesson 3: America Achieves Manifest Destiny 49
Lesson 4: A Religious Awakening Sparks Reform. 50
Lesson 5: The Abolition Movement 52
Lesson 6: Women Work for Change 53
Review Questions 54

Topic 7
Sectional Divisions and the Civil War
Note Taking Study Guide. 56
Lesson 1 Slavery Divides the Nation 57
Lesson 2: Violence Escalates. 59
Lesson 3: The Civil War Begins. 61
Lesson 4: African Americans and the War. . 63
Lesson 5: Everyday Life During the War. . . 64
Lesson 6: Key Civil War Battles. 65
Lesson 7: Impact of the Civil War 66
Review Questions 67

Topic 8
Reconstruction
Note Taking Study Guide. 69
Lesson 1: Plans for Reconstruction Clash . . 70
Lesson 2: Reconstruction Changes the South. 71

Copyright © by Pearson Education, Inc., or its affiliates. All Rights Reserved.

Lesson 3: Reconstruction's Impact 73
Review Questions 75

Topic 9
Industry and Immigration
Note Taking Study Guide................ 76
Lesson 1: Innovation Boosts Growth 77
Lesson 2: Big Business Rises 79
Lesson 3: The Organized Labor
    Movement...................... 81
Lesson 4: The New Immigrants.......... 83
Lesson 5: A Nation of Cities............. 84
Lesson 6: New Ways of Life 85
Review Questions 86

Topic 10
Challenges in the Late 1800s
Note Taking Study Guide................ 88
Lesson 1: American Indians Under
    Pressure........................ 89
Lesson 2: The West Is Transformed........ 90
Lesson 3: Corruption Plagues
    the Nation...................... 91
Lesson 4: Farm Issues and Populism 92
Review Questions 93

Topic 11
America Comes of Age
Note Taking Study Guide................ 94
Lesson 1: Progressives Drive Reform 95
Lesson 2: Women Gain Rights........... 97
Lesson 3: Striving for Equality 98
Lesson 4: Reformers in the White
    House 99
Lesson 5: American Influence Grows..... 101
Lesson 6: The Spanish-American
    War........................... 102
Lesson 7: The United States Emerges
    as a World Power 103
Review Questions 104

Topic 12
World War I and the 1920s
Note Taking Study Guide............... 106
Lesson 1: America Enters World
    War I 107
Lesson 2: The Home Front During
    World War I 108
Lesson 3: The End of World War I 109
Lesson 4: The Postwar Economy
    Booms 110
Lesson 5: Government in the 1920s....... 112
Lesson 6: An Unsettled Society 113
Lesson 7: The Roaring Twenties 114

Lesson 8: The Harlem Renaissance....... 115
Review Questions 116

Topic 13
The Great Depression and the New Deal
Note Taking Study Guide............... 118
Lesson 1: Causes of the Depression 119
Lesson 2: Americans Suffer 120
Lesson 3: Two Presidents Respond....... 121
Lesson 4: The New Deal Expands........ 123
Lesson 5: Effects of the New Deal........ 125
Lesson 6: Culture During the
    Depression 126
Review Questions 127

Topic 14
World War II
Note Taking Study Guide............... 129
Lesson 1: Rise of Aggressive
    Dictators 130
Lesson 2: America Debates
    Involvement................... 131
Lesson 3: America Enters World
    War II......................... 132
Lesson 4: A War on Two Fronts......... 133
Lesson 5: The Home Front 134
Lesson 6: The Allies Win World
    War II......................... 135
Lesson 7: The Holocaust............... 136
Lesson 8: Impact of World War II 137
Review Questions 138

Topic 15
Postwar America
Note Taking Study Guide............... 140
Lesson 1: The Beginning of the
    Cold War...................... 141
Lesson 2: The Korean War 142
Lesson 3: The Cold War Intensifies....... 143
Lesson 4: Cold War Fears at Home....... 144
Lesson 5: Postwar Prosperity........... 145
Lesson 6: Mass Culture in the 1950s...... 147
Lesson 7: Social Issues of the 1950s 148
Review Questions 150

Topic 16
Civil Rights and Reform in the 1960s
Note Taking Study Guide............... 152
Lesson 1: The Civil Rights Movement
    Strengthens.................... 153
Lesson 2: The Movement Surges
    Forward 154
Lesson 3: Successes and Setbacks 155
Lesson 4: Kennedy's Reforms 156

Lesson 5: Reform Under Johnson 157
Review Questions 158

Topic 17
The Vietnam War Era
Note Taking Study Guide............... 160
Lesson 1: The Cold War and Vietnam 161
Lesson 2: America's Role Escalates...... 163
Lesson 3: The Antiwar Movement 164
Lesson 4: The War's End and Effects 165
Review Questions 166

Topic 18
An Era of Change
Note Taking Study Guide............... 167
Lesson 1: The Counterculture of the
    1960s 168
Lesson 2: The Women's Rights
    Movement......................... 169
Lesson 3: Expanding the Push for
    Equality.......................... 170
Lesson 4: The Environmental
    Movement......................... 171
Lesson 5: The Two Sides of the Nixon
    Presidency 172
Lesson 6: Ford and Carter Struggle 174
Review Questions 176

Topic 19
America in the 1980s and 1990s
Note Taking Study Guide................ 178
Lesson 1: The Conservative
    Movement Surges 179
Lesson 2: The Reagan Era............... 180
Lesson 3: The Cold War Ends 181
Lesson 4: A New Era in Foreign
    Policy............................ 182
Lesson 5: Clinton and the 1990s 183
Review Questions 185

Topic 20
America in the Twenty-First Century
Note Taking Study Guide............... 187
Lesson 1: America and the World
    Economy.......................... 188
Lesson 2: The George W. Bush
    Presidency 189
Lesson 3: The Barack Obama
    Presidency 190
Lesson 4: Americans Look to the
    Future 191
Review Questions 192

How to use the *Reading and Note Taking Study Guide*

The **Reading and Note Taking Study Guide** will help you better understand the content of Pearson *United States History*. This section will also develop your reading, vocabulary, and note taking skills. Each study guide consists of three components. The first component focuses on developing graphic organizers that will help you take notes as you read.

Name _____ Class _____ Date _____

TOPIC 2 — Note Taking Study Guide
ENGLAND'S AMERICAN COLONIES

Focus Question: How were the three regions of English colonies in the 1600s similar and different? What kinds of experiences did colonists have in each region?

As you read, focus on the regions where England established or acquired colonies in the 1600s. Describe their foundation, their religious and political characteristics, their economies, and their relationships with Native Americans.

	Southern Colonies	New England Colonies	Middle Colonies
Founding	•	•	•
Religion	•	•	•
Political / Government	•	•	•
Economy	•	•	•
Relations with Indians	•	•	•

The **Focus Question** gives you a tool to focus your reading.

Each **Note Taking Study Guide** has one graphic organizer for every topic. Completing the graphic organizer will help you comprehend the material and retain important details. Use your completed graphic organizer to review and prepare for assessments.

The second component highlights the central themes, issues, and concepts of each lesson.

Name _____ Class _____ Date _____

TOPIC 2 LESSON 2
Lesson Summary
NEW LIVES IN NEW ENGLAND

MODIFIED CORNELL NOTES

Most of the New England colonists were religious dissidents. Known as Puritans, they wanted to purify the Church of England, which they believed retained too many ceremonies from the Catholic Church. Other dissidents, called Separatists, began their own churches. Puritans believed that they could prepare for God's saving grace by leading moral lives and that salvation depended on the will of God. Puritans came from all ranks of English society. Most of them were farmers, shopkeepers, and skilled artisans. They were persecuted for challenging England's official church. Some Puritans sought a colonial refuge.

In 1620, the first Puritan emigrants, who were later called Pilgrims, crossed the Atlantic in the ship the *Mayflower* to found the Plymouth Colony on the south shore of Massachusetts Bay. Before they disembarked, they made the Mayflower Compact, in which they agreed to form a government and obey its laws. This idea of self-government would become one of the founding principles of the United States. In 1630, a much larger group of Puritans settled the town of Boston. Their leader, John Winthrop, urged them to make their colony an inspirational example for the mother country. From Plymouth and Boston, colonists spread rapidly along the coast and into the interior, settling New Hampshire, Maine, Rhode Island, and Connecticut.

The Puritans in New England did not champion religious **toleration**. During the 1630s, Roger Williams and Anne Hutchinson angered the authorities by arguing that Massachusetts had not done enough to break with Anglican ways. They fled to Rhode Island, which became a rare **haven** for religious toleration. The Rhode Islanders also agreed to separate church and state.

The colonists viewed the Indians as lazy savages. They tried to subdue, convert, and transform the Indians into replicas of English Christians in special "praying towns." In 1675, a massive Indian rebellion erupted. The colonists called it King Philip's War, after a chief named Metacom, who was known to the colonists as "King Philip." The defeated Indians lost most of their remaining lands in southern New England. In 1700, the 92,000 colonists outnumbered New England's 9,000 Indians.

Lesson Vocabulary
toleration government acceptance of religious beliefs and ideas that are different from established ones
haven a safe place

Each **Summary** highlights **Key Terms** in boldface, and summarizes the key points in the lesson.

Use the **Notes** in the side column to record important information from the summary as you read.

The **Lesson Vocabulary** section defines some key terms used in the summary.

The third component consists of review questions that assess your understanding of the lesson.

Name _____ Class _____ Date _____

TOPIC 2 Review Questions
ENGLAND'S AMERICAN COLONIES

Answer the questions below using the information in the Lesson Summaries on the previous pages.

Lesson 1: The Southern Colonies Take Root

1. What finally enabled the colony of Jamestown to thrive?
   _____
   _____

2. **Sequence** List in chronological order the colonies that formed between 1632 and 1732. Provide the date each colony was established.
   _____
   _____
   _____

Lesson 2: New Lives in New England

3. **Recognize Multiple Causes** Summarize the main reasons the Puritans left England for America.
   _____
   _____

4. How did the New England colonists treat the Native Americans?
   _____
   _____

Lesson 3: The Middle Colonies Thrive

5. How did the Dutch colony of New Netherland become the English colony of New York?
   _____
   _____

6. **Identifying Main Ideas and Details** In what ways did Pennsylvania differ from other colonies?
   _____
   _____

Lesson 4: Immigration and Slavery in the Colonies

7. How did European immigration to the colonies change in the late 1600s and 1700s?
   _____
   _____

8. **Identify Main Ideas** Why did the practice of slavery develop in the colonies?
   _____
   _____

Comprehension questions assess your understanding of key points from the summaries.

Reading Skill questions ask you to interpret what you have read.

Name _____ Class _____ Date _____

TOPIC 1
Note Taking Study Guide
AMERICA'S CULTURAL ROOTS

Focus Question: What were the cultures that began to interact in the Americas in the late 1400s and early 1500s? What features and events helped shape each culture?

As you read, take notes about the three main cultures that began to interact in the Americas after Europeans arrived. Identify where each culture developed. Then record details about the characteristics of each culture and the historical events that helped shape them.

I.
   A.
      1.
      2.
   B.
      1.
      2.
      3.
   C.
      1.
      2.
      3.

II.
   A.
      1.
      2.
      3.
   B.
      1.
      2.
      3.

III.
   A.
      1.
      2.
   B.
      1.
      2.
   C.
      1.
      2.
      3.
      4.

Copyright © by Pearson Education, Inc., or its affiliates. All Rights Reserved.

Name _____ Class _____ Date _____

TOPIC 1 LESSON 1

Lesson Summary
THE PEOPLES OF THE AMERICAS

MODIFIED CORNELL NOTES

Until recently, most scholars believed that Paleoindians, the first people in the Americas, arrived 15,000 years ago during an **ice age**. Since much of the planet's seawater was frozen and the sea level was lower, hunters crossed a land bridge between Siberia and Alaska. Now, some scholars theorize that the first Americans migrated, or traveled, from Asia some 40,000 years ago.

About 12,000 to 10,000 years ago, the climate warmed, allowing the environment to become more diverse. Wild plants were domesticated and grown for food. The expanded food supply encouraged population growth, which led to larger, permanent villages. In Mexico, some villages grew into great cities ruled by powerful chiefs. Along the Gulf of Mexico and the Caribbean coast, the leading peoples were the Olmecs and later the Mayas. In the highlands of central Mexico, the Aztecs became the most powerful people. In the Southwest, the Hohokam and the Anasazi built villages and houses of **adobe**, a type of sun-dried brick.

The people who lived in the Mississippi River valley enjoyed a humid and temperate climate. These Mississippians built large towns and developed trade. During the ninth century, some Mississippians moved westward onto the Great Plains, an immense, windy, and **arid** grassland. They built villages, planted crops, and hunted bison in mobile camps. These Great Plains villagers sometimes clashed with hunting **nomads** from the Rocky Mountains.

The Choctaws, Creeks, and other southeastern groups were primarily farmers, but they also depended on hunting and fishing. Northeastern people developed into two major language groups: the Algonquians and the Iroquoians. Five Iroquois people united to form the Iroquois League, a ritual forum for promoting peaceful cooperation among the members.

Despite their cultural diversity, most American Indian groups shared several cultural features. American Indians believed that spirits could be found in every plant, animal, rock, cloud, and body of water. They possessed little private property and maintained a respectful equality among the various groups of Indians.

Lesson Vocabulary

ice age period in Earth's history with low global temperatures and glaciers covering large areas

adobe sun-dried brick made from earth, water, and straw

arid very dry; having little rain or water

nomads people who move from place to place instead of staying and settling in one place

Name _____ Class _____ Date _____

TOPIC 1 LESSON 2

Lesson Summary
THE WEST AFRICANS

MODIFIED CORNELL NOTES

West Africa is a diverse land with valuable **natural resources** such as salt and gold. Hundreds of years ago, these resources formed the basis of trade among the people in West Africa. Trade revolved around trading centers, which grew into great and powerful empires with rich and thriving cultures.

The kingdom of Ghana, running from the Atlantic Ocean to the Niger River, rose to prominence around A.D. 800. By the eleventh century, Ghana supplied much of the gold for the Mediterranean region. Attacks by outsiders weakened Ghana, and the new kingdom of Mali replaced Ghana around A.D. 1200. In the early 1300s, Mali's famous king Mansa Musa expanded Mali's domain westward to the Atlantic coast and increased the role of Islam within the empire. By the 1400s, Mali was eclipsed by the rise of Songhai.

In West Africa, land was not held by individuals as private property. Instead, it belonged to extended kinship networks. Slavery was common and an important part of West Africa's economic foundation. Owning slaves (or wives) rather than property determined one's wealth. Humans were used as items of trade along with gold, salt, ivory, and other resources. Slaves were usually adopted by the families into which they were sold. They were allowed to marry, and their children did not inherit the status of slaves. Most importantly, slavery was not based on the notion of racial inferiority.

As Portuguese explorers made voyage after voyage along the coast of Africa, they discovered a profitable **enterprise**: trade with the people of West Africa. To conduct their African trade, the Portuguese mariners received the assent of the powerful West African kings. The Portuguese greatly expanded the slave trade. By 1500, Europeans purchased about 1,800 African slaves each year. Some were sent to Europe, but most were sent to work on plantations located on the Madeira, Canary, and Azores islands. Thus began the brutal exploitation of West African slaves by Europeans—a fate that would befall millions more African men and women in the centuries ahead.

Lesson Vocabulary

natural resources anything found in nature that is useful to people
enterprise business, or business organization

Name _____ Class _____ Date _____

TOPIC 1 LESSON 3

Lesson Summary
EUROPEANS MAKE CONTACT

MODIFIED CORNELL NOTES

Europe was changing quickly in the 1400s. The Middle Ages, a period marked by limited trade, the absence of strong nations, and little interaction with the outside world, was ending. During the Middle Ages, church leaders sought to ensure that all thought **adhered** to their understanding of the world. In the mid-1400s, the Renaissance brought renewed interest in learning and the arts. Trade with and awareness of the world beyond Europe also expanded, producing wealth and fueling exploration.

Western Europe was divided into warring kingdoms. Each kingdom was ruled by a monarch who let the elite govern. Nearly all land and wealth was held by the elite, who made up less than 5 percent of the population. Three out of five western Europeans were working poor and one tenth to one fifth were beggars.

Many Europeans felt hemmed in by the wealth, power, and technology of their neighbors, the Muslims, who were adherents of Islam rather than Christianity. The Muslims had won a series of religious wars launched by European Christians during the Middle Ages. The Muslim realm stretched across North Africa, around the southern and eastern Mediterranean Sea to parts of eastern Europe and the Middle East. They controlled most of the lucrative trade routes. Inspired by the travel accounts of explorers such as Marco Polo, Europeans dreamed of an alternative trade route around the Muslim world and longed for the fabled riches of India and China.

European expansionists found hope on the Iberian Peninsula. With the 1469 marriage of Prince Ferdinand and Queen Isabella, the kingdoms of Aragon and Castile joined to create the new nation of Spain. They completed the *Reconquista* (reconquest) when Granada, the last Muslim stronghold in Iberia, was seized.

Close to Africa and facing the Atlantic, Spain and Portugal were well placed to lead the maritime expansion of Europe. Portugal took the lead in 1419. Prince Henry, known as Prince Henry the Navigator, became a supporter of oceangoing exploration as a means to spread Christianity and outflank Muslim domination of trade. He helped finance a series of expeditions down the coast of West Africa and founded a school of navigation.

Throughout the 1400s, the Portuguese sought a route around Africa's southern tip into the Indian Ocean. In 1487, the Portuguese mariner Bartolomeu Dias discovered how to use the counterclockwise winds of the South Atlantic to get around southern Africa. In 1498, Vasco de Gama used this discovery to reach India, opening a very profitable channel of trade.

(Continues on the next page.)

Lesson Vocabulary

adhere to follow rules closely or stick firmly to a belief

Copyright © by Pearson Education, Inc., or its affiliates. All Rights Reserved.

Lesson Summary
EUROPEANS MAKE CONTACT (continued)

TOPIC 1, LESSON 3

MODIFIED CORNELL NOTES

Christopher Columbus, an Italian mariner, pursued Spain's dream of westward exploration in the Atlantic Ocean. When Columbus reached the present-day Bahamas and adjacent islands, he mistakenly believed these islands were off the mainland of Asia. He claimed the land for Spain despite the presence of native people.

In 1497, John Cabot, a Genoese mariner, sailed to Newfoundland, and a Portuguese fleet led by Pedro Alvarez Cabral discovered Brazil in 1500. A year later, another Genoese mariner, Amerigo Vespucci, deemed South America a new continent. Between 1519 and 1522, a voyage begun by Ferdinand Magellan circled the entire globe.

In 1519, Hernán Cortés marched to the inland home of the Aztec Empire in Mexico. The Spanish captured the capital city of Tenochtitlán and began building a Spanish capital, Mexico City, on its ruins. The Spanish expanded their empire deep into North and South America. The **conquistadors** were motivated by religious faith and loyalty to their monarch, as well as wealth. European diseases such as smallpox devastated native populations, which had no natural defenses against them. With the death of so many Indians, the colonists turned to African slaves to work the new sugar plantations.

The colonizers also introduced plants and animals that were new to the Americas in what is referred to as the Columbian Exchange. These new plants and animals brought drastic changes to the environment. Europeans also began farming American plants such as maize and potatoes. Large harvests aided by these new American crops fueled European population growth while native populations declined.

Lesson Vocabulary

conquistador   Spanish conqueror

Name _____ Class _____ Date _____

TOPIC 1 LESSON 4
Lesson Summary
SPAIN AND FRANCE IN THE AMERICAS

MODIFIED CORNELL NOTES

Enriched by conquests in the Americas, Spain financed an aggressive military policy in Europe. This aggression alarmed the Dutch, French, and English, who sought their own share of the riches in America. With the spread of the Protestant Reformation, religious divisions added to the conflict among nations in Europe.

The conquistadores were successful at conquering territory but not at running the colonies. Catholic **missionaries** aimed to convert Indians to Christianity and to persuade them to conform to Spanish culture. The missionaries relied on Spanish soldiers, who set up **presidios**, or forts, near the mission.

Spain's American empire was divided into two immense regions, New Spain and Peru. Each was ruled by a **viceroy** appointed by the king. Most of the colonists were men, and many took Indian wives. Their children became known as **mestizos**. The mestizos became the largest segment of Spain's colonial population by the eighteenth century. Next in proportion were enslaved Africans, especially in the Caribbean region. In both New Spain and Peru, the Spanish developed an urban and cosmopolitan culture.

Hernando de Soto and Franciso Vásquez de Coronado led expeditions into the lands north of Mexico. De Soto's men explored present-day Florida and other areas, leaving behind deadly new diseases. Coronado searched for a golden kingdom named Quivara, but found only villages of grass-thatched lodges. After the failures of de Soto and Coronado, the Spanish Crown lost interest in the northern lands. Friars tried to transform Indians into Hispanics by building **missions** in native villages. In New Mexico, the Pueblo Indians would not give up all their traditional beliefs. The missionaries' harsh punishments for these infractions angered the Pueblos.

(Continues on the next page.)

Lesson Vocabulary

missionary   person sent to a foreign country in order to convert others to their religion

presidio   fort built by the Spanish in colonial America, usually in what is today the U.S. Southwest and California

viceroy   in colonial Spanish America, king-appointed official who governs a province, colony, or country

mestizos   people in Spanish colonial America who were of European and Native American decent

missions   religious settlements usually run by Catholic priests and friars in colonial Spanish America

Copyright © by Pearson Education, Inc., or its affiliates. All Rights Reserved.

Lesson Summary
SPAIN AND FRANCE IN THE AMERICAS (continued)

MODIFIED CORNELL NOTES

Conditions worsened during the 1660s and 1670s. A prolonged drought undercut the harvests, reducing many Pueblos to starvation. In 1680, the Pueblos revolted under the leadership of a shaman named Popé. The rebels destroyed and plundered missions, farms, and ranches. The Pueblo Revolt was the greatest setback that the Indians ever inflicted on colonial expansion. After Popé's death, the Spanish reclaimed New Mexico. The bloody revolt taught the Pueblos and the Spanish to compromise.

During the early 1500s, French explorers wanted to find a Northwest Passage to Asia. They probed the eastern coastline of North America, from present-day North Carolina to Newfoundland. The French king claimed the region around the St. Lawrence River as New France. French mariners fished for cod and hunted for whales and seals. They met Indian hunters who offered beaver fur in trade. The coastal Indians sought new stocks of beaver by invading the hunting territories of their neighbors, provoking wars between Indian groups.

The traders also plundered and killed one another in their competition for furs. To repel rivals, a French company built a fortified trading post on the St. Lawrence River in 1608. Quebec was the first permanent settlement in Canada. Its founder, Samuel de Champlain, traded with the Montagnais, Algonquin, and Huron Indians. In return, they expected Champlain to help them against their foes, the Iroquois, who lived to the south in what is now New York. The Iroquois acquired guns from Dutch traders on the Hudson River, becoming better armed than their enemies.

New France grew slowly. By 1700, the colony had only 15,000 colonists. Its government resembled that of New Spain. The French king appointed a military governor-general, a civil administrator, and a Catholic bishop. Like the Spanish, the French used Catholic priests as missionaries to convert the Indians. To the west, Indians dominated the vast hinterland of forest and lakes, where the colonists were few and scattered. In the Great Lakes and Illinois countries, the French established some small settlements. They lived by a mix of farming and trade. Many fur traders, known as *coureurs de bois*, married Indian women. The children of these marriages were known as the *metis*.

(Continues on the next page.)

Lesson Vocabulary

coureurs de bois from the French for "runner of the woods," French colonists who lived in the woods as fur traders

metis person in French colonial America who was of French and Native American descent

Name _____ Class _____ Date _____

TOPIC 1 LESSON 4

Lesson Summary
SPAIN AND FRANCE IN THE AMERICAS (continued)

MODIFIED CORNELL NOTES

At the end of the 1600s, the French also established a southern colony along the lower Mississippi Valley. They named this Louisiana, in honor of King Louis XIV. In 1718, they founded New Orleans, which became the colony's largest town and leading seaport. The French valued Louisiana as a military base to keep the English from taking control of the Mississippi watershed.

Name _____ Class _____ Date _____

TOPIC 1: Review Questions
AMERICA'S CULTURAL ROOTS

Answer the questions below using the information in the Lesson Summaries on the previous pages.

Lesson 1: The Peoples of the Americas

1. Describe the theories that scholars have about the arrival of Paleoindians in America.
   _____
   _____

2. **Identify Main Ideas** What cultural features did most Native American groups share?
   _____
   _____

Lesson 2: The West Africans

3. Describe the practice of slavery in West Africa.
   _____
   _____

4. **Identify Details** How did Mansa Musa alter the kingdom of Mali?
   _____
   _____

Lesson 3: Europeans Make Contact

5. **Summarize** Describe how life changed in Europe during the Renaissance.
   _____
   _____

6. Explain why the Europeans felt hemmed in by the trade routes of the Muslim world.
   _____
   _____

Copyright © by Pearson Education, Inc., or its affiliates. All Rights Reserved.

Name _____ Class _____ Date _____

TOPIC 1
Review Questions
AMERICA'S CULTURAL ROOTS (continued)

Lesson 4: Spain and France in the Americas

7. How did Spain organize its American empire?
_____
_____

8. **Compare and Contrast** How were Spanish America and New France alike and how were they different?
_____
_____

Name _____ Class _____ Date _____

TOPIC 2
Note Taking Study Guide
ENGLAND'S AMERICAN COLONIES

Focus Question: How were the three regions of English colonies in the 1600s similar and different? What kinds of experiences did colonists have in each region?

As you read, focus on the regions where England established or acquired colonies in the 1600s. Describe their foundation, their religious and political characteristics, their economies, and their relationships with Native Americans.

	Southern Colonies	New England Colonies	Middle Colonies
Founding	•	•	•
Religion	•	•	•
Political / Government	•	•	•
Economy	•	•	•
Relations with Indians	•	•	•

Copyright © by Pearson Education, Inc., or its affiliates. All Rights Reserved.

Name _____ Class _____ Date _____

TOPIC 2 LESSON 1

Lesson Summary
THE SOUTHERN COLONIES TAKE ROOT

MODIFIED CORNELL NOTES

The first English colonies were promoted by wealthy gentlemen who obtained a **charter**, or certificate of permission, from the king. Then, the group formed a **joint-stock company** run by several investors. During the 1580s, Sir Walter Raleigh twice tried to colonize Roanoke, a small island on the North Carolina coast. In 1607, the Virginia Company established a colony on Chesapeake Bay, a region that offered many good harbors and navigable rivers, as well as more fertile land. A powerful American Indian chief named Powhatan hoped to use the English against his own enemies and to trade for their metal weapons. The colonists, led by Captain John Smith, wanted Indian lands.

The new settlement was named Jamestown to honor the king. By taking food from the Indians, the colonists provoked conflicts. By 1616, the colony was an unprofitable town of 350 diseased, hungry, and unhappy colonists. Then the planters learned how to cultivate tobacco, and the profits attracted more immigrants to Virginia. Under the headright system, anyone paying passage to Virginia received 50 acres of land. In 1619, the Virginia Company allowed the planters to create the House of Burgesses, the first representative body in colonial America. It had the power to make laws and raise taxes. In 1624, Virginia became the first royal colony in the English empire. **Royal colonies** belonged to the Crown, while **proprietary colonies** belonged to powerful individuals or companies.

In 1675, intense fighting erupted between the Indians and the settlers in the Potomac Valley. When the royal governor of Virginia, William Berkeley, protested the slaughter of Indians, Nathaniel Bacon marched his armed followers to Jamestown in a revolt called Bacon's Rebellion. Although the rebellion collapsed, it undermined Berkeley's credibility.

In 1632, a second colony, Maryland, was established at the northern head of Chesapeake Bay. Charles I gave Maryland to Lord Baltimore, who owned and governed it as a proprietary colony. He provided refuge for his fellow Catholics, who were discriminated against in England. In 1670, the English established Carolina south of Virginia. In 1691, they set aside the northern half of their territory as the distinct colony of North Carolina. Georgia was founded in 1732 as a proprietary colony. Its leader, James Oglethorpe, wanted to make Georgia a haven for English debtors.

Lesson Vocabulary

charter legal document giving certain rights to a person or company
joint-stock company a company run by a small group of investors who share the company's profits and losses
royal colony English colony that was under direct control of the Crown
proprietary colony English colony granted to an individual or group by the Crown

Name _____ Class _____ Date _____

TOPIC 2 LESSON 2
Lesson Summary
NEW LIVES IN NEW ENGLAND

MODIFIED CORNELL NOTES

Most of the New England colonists were religious dissidents. Known as Puritans, they wanted to purify the Church of England, which they believed retained too many ceremonies from the Catholic Church. Other dissidents, called Separatists, began their own churches. Puritans believed that they could prepare for God's saving grace by leading moral lives and that salvation depended on the will of God. Puritans came from all ranks of English society. Most of them were farmers, shopkeepers, and skilled artisans. They were persecuted for challenging England's official church. Some Puritans sought a colonial refuge.

In 1620, the first Puritan emigrants, who were later called Pilgrims, crossed the Atlantic in the ship the *Mayflower* to found the Plymouth Colony on the south shore of Massachusetts Bay. Before they disembarked, they made the Mayflower Compact, in which they agreed to form a government and obey its laws. This idea of self-government would become one of the founding principles of the United States. In 1630, a much larger group of Puritans settled the town of Boston. Their leader, John Winthrop, urged them to make their colony an inspirational example for the mother country. From Plymouth and Boston, colonists spread rapidly along the coast and into the interior, settling New Hampshire, Maine, Rhode Island, and Connecticut.

The Puritans in New England did not champion religious **toleration**. During the 1630s, Roger Williams and Anne Hutchinson angered the authorities by arguing that Massachusetts had not done enough to break with Anglican ways. They fled to Rhode Island, which became a rare **haven** for religious toleration. The Rhode Islanders also agreed to separate church and state.

The colonists viewed the Indians as lazy savages. They tried to subdue, convert, and transform the Indians into replicas of English Christians in special "praying towns." In 1675, a massive Indian rebellion erupted. The colonists called it King Philip's War, after a chief named Metacom, who was known to the colonists as "King Philip." The defeated Indians lost most of their remaining lands in southern New England. In 1700, the 92,000 colonists outnumbered New England's 9,000 Indians.

Lesson Vocabulary

toleration   government acceptance of religious beliefs and ideas that are different from established ones

haven   a safe place

Name _____ Class _____ Date _____

TOPIC 2 LESSON 3
Lesson Summary
THE MIDDLE COLONIES THRIVE

MODIFIED CORNELL NOTES

Beginning in 1609, Dutch merchant ships sailed across the Atlantic and up the Hudson River to trade for furs with the Indians. In 1614, they founded a permanent settlement at Fort Nassau on the upper river. To guard the mouth of the river, the Dutch built New Amsterdam at the tip of Manhattan Island in 1626. It became the colony's largest town, major seaport, and government headquarters. The Dutch West India Company appointed the governor and an advisory council of leading colonists. New Netherland tolerated various religious groups, including Jews. However, the colony attracted few immigrants. **Push factors** motivate people to leave their home countries, while **pull factors** attract people to a new location. There was less cause for the Dutch to leave home than the English.

In 1638, traders founded New Sweden on the lower Delaware River, within the present state of Delaware. Some of the colonists were Swedes, but most came from Finland. These colonists introduced many frontier techniques that eventually became classically American, such as log cabins. In September 1655, New Sweden was forced to surrender to its Dutch neighbors.

In 1664, the English forced the Dutch governor to surrender New Amsterdam, which the English renamed New York, after its proprietor, the Duke of York. The region between the Chesapeake and New England colonies became known as the Middle Colonies. The Duke of York granted lands between the Hudson and Delaware rivers as a new colony called New Jersey.

Pennsylvania began as a debt paid to William Penn by King Charles II of England. Penn belonged to a **radical** form of Protestantism whose members were called Quakers. They relied on mystical experience to know God and understand the Bible. They considered women spiritually equal to men, refused to bear arms, and tolerated other faiths. In 1680, the king granted to Penn the land west of the Delaware River as the colony of Pennsylvania, or "Penn's Woods." In 1682, Penn arrived and established a city named Philadelphia. Cultivating a peace with the local Indians, the Pennsylvanians avoided the sort of native rebellions that devastated other colonies. In their ethnic and religious pluralism, the Middle Colonies anticipated the diversity of America's future population.

Lesson Vocabulary

push factors   factors that motivate people to leave their home countries

pull factors   factors that attract people to a new location

radical   favoring or making extreme changes in political, social, religious, or economic thought or practice

Copyright © by Pearson Education, Inc., or its affiliates. All Rights Reserved.

Name _____ Class _____ Date _____

Lesson Summary
TOPIC 2 LESSON 4
IMMIGRATION AND SLAVERY IN THE COLONIES

MODIFIED CORNELL NOTES

As the English colonies developed, Europeans began to arrive in greater numbers. In the 1600s, about 90 percent of the migrants came from England. About half of the colonial immigrants were **indentured servants**. Too poor to afford the cost of passage, they paid by agreeing to work for a period of four to seven years. Instead of receiving a wage, they received food, clothing, and shelter.

After 1660, English emigration decreased, but Scottish emigration soared. Generally poorer than the English, the Scots had more reasons to seek their fortunes elsewhere. Germans were second only to the Scots-Irish as immigrants to British America. Most of the German immigrants were Protestant, seeking to escape war, taxes, and religious persecution.

Immigration made colonial society more diverse. Although the different groups often distrusted one another at first, they all gradually accepted that a diverse society was an economic boon and the best guarantee for their own faith.

As the number of indentured servants declined in the late 1600s, many colonists turned to another source of labor: enslaved Africans. By law, the position as slave was passed from parent to child. This change in legal **status** promoted the racist idea that people of African origin were inferior to whites. Once firmly established in the colonies, slavery expanded rapidly. Enslaved Africans came to the Americas as part of a three-part voyage called the **triangular trade**. In the Middle Passage, shippers carried the enslaved Africans across the Atlantic to the American colonies. The brutality of the Middle Passage was extreme, and at least 10 percent of those making the trip in the 1700s did not survive.

Slavery varied considerably by region. In 1750, slaves made up small minorities in New England and the Middle Colonies. Many more slaves lived in the Southern Colonies, where they raised labor-intensive crops of tobacco, rice, indigo, or sugar. A lifetime of enslavement was the fate of most African Americans, but some did obtain their freedom. A rare few, such as Phillis Wheatley, managed to overcome enormous obstacles to distinguish themselves.

Lesson Vocabulary

indentured servant   individual who agreed to work without wages for a period of time in exchange for transportation to the colonies

status   legal position or condition of a person, group, country, etc.

triangular trade   the three-way pattern of trade that involved England, English colonies in the Americas, and West Africa

MODIFIED CORNELL NOTES

TOPIC 2 LESSON 5
Lesson Summary
ECONOMIC AND SOCIAL LIFE IN THE COLONIES

In the mid-1600s, Parliament passed a series of trade laws in order to control colonial commerce. The Navigation Acts stated that only English ships with English sailors could trade with English colonies. These acts expressed an economic philosophy known as **mercantilism**, which holds that a nation can build wealth and power by developing its industries and exporting manufactured goods in exchange for gold and silver. The Navigation Acts promoted the dramatic growth of English colonial commerce. The expanding transatlantic commerce produced a "consumer revolution" that brought more and cheaper goods to the colonies.

By the mid-1700s, the colonies had developed important regional distinctions based on geography and climate. New England has cold winters, a short growing season, and a rugged landscape. Most New Englanders worked small farms where they raised livestock and grew wheat, rye, corn, and potatoes for their own use. Since none of these commodities could profitably be shipped to England, they exported lumber and fish and used their abundant woods to build ships.

As in New England, family farms prevailed in the Middle Colonies. However, their farms were more prosperous than those to the north. A more temperate climate allowed farmers to produce and export wheat. The Middle Colonies boomed during the eighteenth century.

Because of a warm climate and long growing season, the Southern Colonies could raise the most valuable and profitable colonial crops. In Virginia and Maryland, planters raised **staple crops**, such as tobacco, which were in steady demand. These crops were also **cash crops**, crops grown for sale. North Carolina produced cattle and lumber, while South Carolina and Georgia harvested rice and indigo.

The three colonial regions also varied in the shape and form of social life that developed there. European immigrants seemed to prefer the Middle Colonies, which became the most ethnically and culturally diverse region in the entire British Empire. In addition to religious tolerance, the Middle Colonies offered immigrants greater economic opportunities.

(Continues on the next page.)

Lesson Vocabulary

mercantilism   economic policy under which a nation accumulates wealth by exporting more goods than it imports

staple crops   basic crop grown in a region

cash crops   a crop grown for sale

TOPIC 2 LESSON 5

Lesson Summary
ECONOMIC AND SOCIAL LIFE IN THE COLONIES (continued)

MODIFIED CORNELL NOTES

Though a less desirable destination for immigrants, New England provided a healthier environment. New England was free of the malaria and dysentery that killed so many colonists elsewhere, allowing the population to grow rapidly. New England leaders favored compact settlement in towns to support public schools and to sustain local churches. By law and custom, there were few opportunities for women outside the home. Some girls received an education in **dame schools**, private schools operated out of a woman's home. Outside of New England, education was less widely available.

In the Southern Colonies, the plantation economy based on slavery produced great profits at the expense of cultural development and economic opportunity. A few white people became rich planters, but most remained common farmers.

Lesson Vocabulary

dame school an elementary school during colonial times, often operated out of a woman's home

Name _____ Class _____ Date _____

Topic 2, Lesson 6 — Lesson Summary
CREATING AN AMERICAN IDENTITY

MODIFIED CORNELL NOTES

Compared with the Spanish or French rulers, the English monarch exercised little direct control over the colonists. The English monarchs were bound to uphold the provisions of the Magna Carta. This document limited the king's ability to tax nobles; it also guaranteed due process, or the right to a trial. During the 1300s, the lawmaking body known as Parliament evolved.

Most settlers in the English colonies **asserted** that they were entitled to the same rights as any other English subject. In 1689, the colonists learned that James II had been overthrown in England. The new monarchs signed an English Bill of Rights guaranteeing a number of freedoms, including that of **habeas corpus**—the idea that no one can be held in prison without being charged with a specific crime. The Glorious Revolution encouraged England to adopt a policy of **salutary neglect**, which allowed its colonies virtual self-rule.

During the 1600s and 1700s, Europe experienced an intellectual movement known as the Enlightenment. It challenged old ways of thinking about science, religion, and government. Enlightenment ideas changed the way American colonists such as Benjamin Franklin viewed the world as well. The colonists' outlook was also shaped by a new movement of heightened religious fervor, known as the Great Awakening. Preachers such as Jonathan Edwards and George Whitefield stressed an emotional and deeply personal religious experience. The Great Awakening inspired the American people with a sense of their own power as individuals. It also led many colonists to believe that if they could choose their method of worship, they could decide on their form of government.

Lesson Vocabulary

assert to state positively; to declare

habeas corpus a constitutional guarantee that no one can be held in prison without charges being filed

salutary neglect a British policy in early 1700s that allowed the colonies virtual self-rule as long as Great Britain profited economically

Copyright © by Pearson Education, Inc., or its affiliates. All Rights Reserved.

Name _____ Class _____ Date _____

TOPIC 2 Review Questions
ENGLAND'S AMERICAN COLONIES

Answer the questions below using the information in the Lesson Summaries on the previous pages.

Lesson 1: The Southern Colonies Take Root

1. What finally enabled the colony of Jamestown to thrive?
_____
_____

2. Sequence List in chronological order the colonies that formed between 1632 and 1732. Provide the date each colony was established.
_____
_____
_____

Lesson 2: New Lives in New England

3. Recognize Multiple Causes Summarize the main reasons the Puritans left England for America.
_____
_____
_____

4. How did the New England colonists treat the Native Americans?
_____
_____
_____

Lesson 3: The Middle Colonies Thrive

5. How did the Dutch colony of New Netherland become the English colony of New York?
_____
_____

6. Identifying Main Ideas and Details In what ways did Pennsylvania differ from other colonies?
_____
_____
_____

Lesson 4: Immigration and Slavery in the Colonies

7. How did European immigration to the colonies change in the late 1600s and 1700s?
_____
_____

8. Identify Main Ideas Why did the practice of slavery develop in the colonies?
_____
_____

Name _____ Class _____ Date _____

TOPIC 2 — Review Questions
ENGLAND'S AMERICAN COLONIES (continued)

Lesson 5: Economic and Social Life in the Colonies

9. What did the Middle Colonies offer immigrants?
_____
_____

10. **Compare and Contrast** How did climate affect the economies of New England and the Middle Colonies?
_____
_____

Lesson 6: Creating an American Identity

11. How did most settlers in the English colonies view themselves in relation to England?
_____
_____

12. **Cause and Effect** How did the Great Awakening affect Americans?
_____
_____

Name _____ Class _____ Date _____

TOPIC 3
Note Taking Study Guide
THE AMERICAN REVOLUTION

Focus Question: What key events helped determine the course of the American Revolution?

As you read, focus on the key events of the American Revolution. Briefly note each event next to the line marking the year it happened. Some years may include more than one event. Others may not have any events.

|—————|—————|—————|—————|—————|—————|—————|
1775　1776　1777　1778　1779　1780　1781

MODIFIED CORNELL NOTES

TOPIC 3 LESSON 1

Lesson Summary
THE FRENCH AND INDIAN WAR

Between 1689 and 1748, the British and the French fought a series of wars. Each side gave generous gifts to woo the Indians. The Indians recognized the importance of preserving the balance of power between the French and the British. However, that balance began to tip as the British colonial population grew and the French were more restrained, treating most American Indians with respect and generosity. The outnumbered French worked with their Indian allies to resist British colonial expansion.

To discourage British colonists from moving into the rich Ohio River valley, the French built Fort Duquesne. The new fort angered the British governor of Virginia. He sent troops led by George Washington to **evict** the French. They did not succeed, and the incident helped to start the French and Indian War.

The British fared poorly in North America until 1758 and 1759, when they managed to cut off French shipping to the Americas. Many Indians deserted the French in order to receive better goods from the British. In 1760, the British captured Montreal and forced the surrender of the rest of Canada. In 1763, the Treaty of Paris ended the war triumphantly for the British, who kept Canada, the Great Lakes country, the Ohio River valley, and Florida. They had driven the French from North America.

The conquest of Canada was dreadful news to Indians of the interior. During the spring of 1763, members of several Indian groups surprised and captured most of the British forts in the Ohio River valley and along the Great Lakes. Their goal was to weaken the British and lure the French back into North America. Pontiac's Rebellion ended when the Indian nations made peace in return for British promises to **restrain** the settlers. The Proclamation of 1763 ordered colonial settlers to remain east of the Appalachian Mountains.

With British encouragement, colonial delegates met in 1754 to review Benjamin Franklin's Albany Plan of Union. The plan called on the colonies to unite under British rule and cooperate with each other. At the time, none of the colonies would accept the plan for fear of losing some **autonomy**. The British also feared that the united colonies might be even more difficult to manage.

Lesson Vocabulary

evict   to force someone to leave a place

restrain   to hold back from action

autonomy   the independent control over one's own affairs

Name _____ Class _____ Date _____

TOPIC 3 LESSON 2
Lesson Summary
CAUSES OF THE REVOLUTION

MODIFIED CORNELL NOTES

Colonial governments were supposed to be miniature versions of the British government. However, the British constitution was not a formal document but a collection of laws and traditions. In contrast, the colonists' rights were spelled out in written contracts such as the Mayflower Compact or royal charters. Still, members of Parliament saw themselves as "**virtual** representatives" of all British citizens, including the colonists.

After the Seven Years' War, Parliament decided that the colonists should pay more to help the British Empire. The Stamp Act, passed in March 1765, required the colonists to pay a tax on almost all printed materials. This was the first time that Parliament had imposed a direct tax on the colonies. The colonists protested angrily. Patrick Henry of Virginia argued that only the colonial assemblies had the right to tax the colonists. Those who opposed the British taxes began to call themselves "Patriots." To lead the protests, some men joined together as the Sons of Liberty.

In 1767, Parliament passed the Townshend Acts, which levied new import duties on items such as glass and tea. When riots broke out in Boston, the Crown sent in 4,000 troops. In March 1770, soldiers fired into a crowd, killing five colonists. Patriots called the killings the Boston Massacre. They formed **committees of correspondence** to provide leadership and promote cooperation. The British withdrew their troops from Boston but kept the tax on tea. On December 16, 1773, the Boston Sons of Liberty dressed as Indians and boarded three British ships laden with tea, which they dumped into the harbor. The event became known as the Boston Tea Party.

To punish Boston, Parliament passed the Coercive Acts, which became known as the Intolerable Acts. These acts closed the port of Boston and forced colonists to house British troops. Leaders from other colonies watched the situation in Boston closely. In the fall of 1774, delegates from every colony except Georgia met in Philadelphia, Pennsylvania, for the First Continental Congress. They announced a boycott of all British imports and established new governments that bypassed the Parliament and the Crown.

Lesson Vocabulary

virtual   being such in practice or effect, though not in actual fact; implied

committees of correspondence   network of local groups that informed colonists of British measures and the opposition to them in the years before the Revolutionary War

Copyright © by Pearson Education, Inc., or its affiliates. All Rights Reserved.

Name _____ Class _____ Date _____

MODIFIED CORNELL NOTES

TOPIC 3 LESSON 3

Lesson Summary
THE COLONISTS DECLARE INDEPENDENCE

On April 19, 1775, war erupted with battles at Lexington and Concord, small towns west of Boston. British troops that had been sent to seize Patriot weapons **stockpiled** in Concord encountered the Patriot **militia**, full-time farmers who were part-time soldiers. The British were pushed back to Boston, and provincial assemblies of Patriots seized control of the New England colonies. **Loyalists**, or colonists who remained loyal to Britain, fled to take refuge with the British troops in Boston. In May 1775, delegates from all the colonies assembled in Philadelphia for the Second Continental Congress. The Congress assumed responsibility for the war and gave the command of the new Continental Army to George Washington.

Most colonists supported the actions of the Continental Congress, but a large minority preferred British rule. The Loyalists feared that the resistance would lead to a deadly and destructive war that Britain would certainly win. According to **stereotype**, Loyalists were wealthy elitists. In reality, many were ordinary farmers and artisans.

In January 1776, Thomas Paine published a pamphlet called *Common Sense* in which he made a radical proposal: independence from Britain, a republican government, and a union of the colonies. Paine argued that ordinary people should elect their entire government. Although the colonies had enormous social and economic differences, Paine insisted that Americans could create a model that would inspire common people everywhere.

By the spring of 1776, Paine's ideas had built momentum for American independence. Congress selected a committee to draft a document declaring American independence. On July 4, Congress approved the Declaration of Independence. Drafted by Thomas Jefferson, it drew on Paine's ideas to denounce the king. Congress embraced the Enlightenment ideas that all men are born with **natural rights** that cannot be taken away by a government. Jefferson called them "inalienable rights." However, to achieve independence, the poorly organized colonists would have to fight against one of the strongest military powers on Earth.

Lesson Vocabulary

stockpile to gather a large supply of something, such as weapons or food

militia trained citizens who serve as soldiers during an emergency

Loyalists colonists who remained loyal to Britain during the Revolution

stereotype an oversimplified image of a group or people

natural rights universal rights, such as life and liberty that derive from nature rather than a government, according to philosophers

Lesson Summary
TOPIC 3 LESSON 4 — AMERICANS WIN THE REVOLUTION

MODIFIED CORNELL NOTES

Britain seemed to have great advantages at the beginning of the war, which led the British to underestimate the Patriots as an enemy. In 1775, British soldiers under Lord William Howe tried to take the hills overlooking Boston. Although they succeeded, they suffered more than twice the Patriot casualties. Six months later, Patriot reinforcements arrived with cannons they had captured, and the British were forced to abandon the city in March 1776.

The British never fully understood that they were fighting a revolutionary war. They further angered colonists by hiring German **mercenaries**. Patriot persistence owed much to the leadership of George Washington and his use of guerilla warfare and unorthodox tactics to hold off the British. Continental troops worked with local militias and relied on the aid and support of the civilian population.

After leaving Boston, the British attacked New York City to cut off New England from the rest of the colonies. Howe captured the city on September 15. After a modest victory at the Battle of Trenton, Washington began 1777 with another victory when he inflicted heavy casualties on General Charles Cornwallis's troops at the Battle of Princeton. After a Patriot victory at Saratoga, Benjamin Franklin secured help in February 1778. France agreed to become an **ally** of the Patriots. Some French volunteers, including the Marquis de Lafayette, were already providing military expertise. Washington's army spent a harsh winter at Valley Forge outside of Philadelphia. Despite their hardships, the soldiers benefited from drilling exercises supervised by a German officer. The Continental soldiers demonstrated their improved discipline at Monmouth, New Jersey, in June 1778. The outbreak of war between the colonists and the British **escalated** the frequent skirmishes between settlers and Indians. Most Indians sided with the British, who had promised to keep the colonists in the east. American Indians and white settlers increasingly attacked each other, beginning a cycle of revenge that continued for years.

(Continues on the next page.)

Lesson Vocabulary

mercenary   professional soldier who is paid to fight in a foreign army

ally   a person, group, or country that has joined with another to achieve a common purpose

escalate   to make something worse or more severe

Name _____ Class _____ Date _____

TOPIC 3 LESSON 4

Lesson Summary
AMERICANS WIN THE REVOLUTION (continued)

MODIFIED CORNELL NOTES

The British knew they would find more Loyalist support in the South. They won most of the battles and captured the leading seaports, yet failed to control the southern countryside. In October 1780 at Kings Mountain in North Carolina, the Patriots crushed a Loyalist militia. As the Loyalists lost men and territory, neutral civilians swung over to the Patriot side, which **frustrated** the British. During the summer of 1781, Washington marched most of his troops south. He planned to trap Cornwallis's army at Yorktown, Virginia. The French fleet arrived at just the right moment, trapping the British navy. Cornwallis surrendered his army on October 19. The British negotiated a peace treaty with an American delegation led by Benjamin Franklin. The Treaty of Paris recognized American independence and granted generous boundaries to the United States.

Some Americans won far more rights than others. About 90,000 Loyalists—including 20,000 former slaves—became refugees. About half of them resettled in Britain's northern colonies. During the Revolutionary War, the Americans fought on their western frontier to defeat the American Indians. When the British abandoned the Indians in 1783, the Patriots forced the Indians to give up massive tracts of land as the price of peace. Women gained few political or legal rights as a result of the Revolution, but they won greater respect based on the new conception of women as "republican mothers."

African Americans were excluded from the rights demanded by the Patriots. After the war, the Revolution led to emancipation in the North, where slavery was not critical to the economy. Emancipation was much less likely to occur in the South, where slaves were essential to the plantation economy. In Maryland and Virginia, many planters voluntarily freed their slaves, a practice known as **manumission**. After 1810, however, southern states passed laws to discourage further manumissions.

Perhaps the greatest effect of the Revolution was the spreading of the idea of liberty, both at home and abroad. Over the next three centuries, the principles for which the Patriots fought would inspire revolutions around the world, beginning with the French Revolution.

Lesson Vocabulary

frustrate   unable to achieve an objective
manumission   the act of freeing someone from slavery

Name _____ Class _____ Date _____

TOPIC 3 Review Questions
THE AMERICAN REVOLUTION

Answer the questions below using the information in the Lesson Summaries on the previous pages.

Lesson 1: The French and Indian War

1. Why did many American Indian groups fight alongside the French?
_____
_____

2. **Recognize Sequence** What event led many American Indians to desert the French in favor of the British?
_____
_____

Lesson 2: Causes of the Revolution

3. **Recognize Sequence** What event led to the first eruption of violence between the colonists and English troops?
_____
_____

4. What was the significance of the First Continental Congress?
_____
_____

Lesson 3: The Colonists Declare Independence

5. How did the Second Continental Congress respond to the beginning of the war?
_____
_____

6. **Identify Cause and Effect** What role did the publication of *Common Sense* play in leading the colonies to declare their independence?
_____
_____

Lesson 4: Americans Win the Revolution

7. How did the American Revolution affect African Americans?
_____
_____

8. **Identify Cause and Effect** What effect did the American Revolution have on other parts of the world?
_____
_____

Name _____ Class _____ Date _____

Note Taking Study Guide
TOPIC 4 — ESTABLISHING THE NEW NATION

Focus Question: How was the government established by the Constitution different from the government established by the Articles of Confederation? How was it the same?

As you read, focus on the similarities and differences between the government established by the Articles of Confederation and the government established by the Constitution. Note what kind of government each one was, what officials it included, and what powers it had. Record any elements the two governments had in common in the area where the two circles overlap.

Articles of Confederation | **Constitution**

Name _____ Class _____ Date _____

TOPIC 4 LESSON 1

Lesson Summary
THE ARTICLES OF CONFEDERATION

MODIFIED CORNELL NOTES

Upon declaring independence in 1776, the Congress invited each new state to create a constitution. The constitutions all called for **republics**, or governments in which officials are representatives elected by the people. The more liberal Patriots preferred a **unicameral legislature**, or a single house elected by the people. Most states chose to create state governments made up of a **bicameral legislature**, a lawmaking body with two houses—a Senate and a House of Representatives. In most states, conservatives preserved colonial property requirements for voting. Most state constitutions guaranteed freedom of religion.

In 1777, the Continental Congress drafted the Articles of Confederation, the new constitution for the union of the states. Under the leadership of John Dickinson, Congress designed a loose confederation of states rather than a centralized nation. The new **federal**, or national, government included no executive branch. However, the powers to make, **implement**, and enforce the laws were placed with the Congress.

The national Congress created plans for settling and governing the Northwest Territory, the territory north of the Ohio River and west of Pennsylvania to the Mississippi River. In the Land Ordinance of 1785, the Congress designed a system for distributing the public lands. The Northwest Ordinance of 1787 provided a government for the western territory, as well as a process for statehood. Slavery was barred from the territory.

Spain and Britain did not take the new United States seriously. Spain forbade American trade with Spanish-held New Orleans. Britain imposed restrictions that hurt American shipping interests. Britain also kept its forts on American territory.

The weaknesses of the Articles of Confederation contributed to the troubles of the fledgling government. Under the Articles, the federal Congress could not establish a common currency, regulate interstate commerce, or levy taxes. Meanwhile, most Americans were farmers, and most farmers were in debt. They faced the loss of their crops, livestock, and even their farms to foreclosure. In 1786, the Massachusetts army suppressed an uprising by farmers that became known as Shays' Rebellion. Most Americans hoped to save the Republic by establishing a stronger national government.

Lesson Vocabulary

republic   form of government in which representatives and leaders are elected by the people

unicameral legislature   a lawmaking body made up of a single house

bicameral legislature   a lawmaking body made up of two houses

federal   national

implement   to carry into effect

Copyright © by Pearson Education, Inc., or its affiliates. All Rights Reserved.

Name _____ Class _____ Date _____

MODIFIED CORNELL NOTES

TOPIC 4 LESSON 2
Lesson Summary
THE CONSTITUTIONAL CONVENTION

By 1787, it was clear that the Articles of Confederation needed major changes. Most agreed that Congress should have the power to regulate interstate and international commerce and to tax the people. To draft amendments to the Articles, 12 of the 13 states sent delegates to a convention in Philadelphia. Two of the convention's leading thinkers were Alexander Hamilton and James Madison.

During the **subsequent** weeks and months, delegates debated a number of proposals for the new constitution. Most of the delegates favored a scheme proposed by Madison called the Virginia Plan. The plan proposed creating a government that divided power among the legislative, executive, and judicial branches. The plan would establish a bicameral legislature with a House of Representatives and a Senate. In both houses, representation would be based on population. The Virginia Plan also called for a strong President and gave the Congress the power to veto any state law.

The New Jersey Plan proposed only modest changes and was favored by the small states. This plan gave the Congress the power to regulate commerce and to tax, but it kept the three chief principles of the Articles: a unicameral legislature representing the states as equals, an executive committee rather than a President, and **sovereignty** for the states in most areas.

Led by Roger Sherman, the delegates worked out a compromise between the Virginia and the New Jersey plans, known as the Great Compromise. The Senate would equally represent every state by allowing two senators per state. The House of Representatives would represent states based on population, granting more power to the more populous states. The delegates supported a system known as **federalism**, which divided government power between the national and state governments.

During the debates, the delegates discovered that slavery was their greatest division. A compromise known as the Three-Fifths Compromise counted each slave as three fifths of a person to be added to a state's free population in allocating representatives to the House of Representatives and electoral college votes.

Lesson Vocabulary

subsequent following; coming after
sovereign to be independent and self-governing
federalism political system in which power is shared between the national government and state governments

Lesson Summary
TOPIC 4 LESSON 3: THE ENDURING CONSTITUTION

MODIFIED CORNELL NOTES

The delegates to the Constitutional Convention drafted a new constitution. After being signed, the proposed Constitution was printed, circulated, and hotly debated. The delegates ruled that nine states had to **ratify** the new Constitution in specially elected conventions. Two groups emerged in the debate: the Federalists, who supported ratification, and the Antifederalists, who opposed it.

The Federalists argued that a strong central government could overcome the difficulties facing the new nation. The checks and balances in the proposed Constitution would prevent any of the three branches from gaining too much power. The Antifederalists disliked the lack of a bill of rights. They believed that liberty could not survive unless the federal government was weak.

The proposed Constitution lacked majority support in 1787. However, the Constitution had the support of George Washington and Benjamin Franklin, two of the most trusted men in America. The case for ratification of the Constitution was set forth in *The Federalist*, a series of 85 essays written by Madison, Hamilton, and John Jay. These essays were published in New York newspapers in 1787 and 1788.

The Federalists pushed for ratifying conventions in five states and won ratification in all of them. The promise of a bill of rights helped the Federalists to win most of the remaining states. The resistance of the Antifederalists obliged the Federalists to make the concession to add the Bill of Rights, the first ten amendments to the Constitution that provide basic rights. In 1789, the new Congress **convened** in New York City.

(Continues on the next page.)

Lesson Vocabulary

ratify   formally approve

convene   to meet or assemble

Name _____ Class _____ Date _____

TOPIC 4 LESSON 3

Lesson Summary
THE ENDURING CONSTITUTION (continued)

MODIFIED CORNELL NOTES

The writers of the Constitution created an indirect democracy in which voters elect representatives to govern. Similarly, an **electoral college**, or group of persons chosen from each state, indirectly elects the President. The Constitution established a representative government based on these basic principles: **popular sovereignty**, **limited government**, **separation of powers**, federalism, and **checks and balances**. The Constitution has survived, in part, because it provides a process for its own amendment.

Lesson Vocabulary

electoral college   a group of persons chosen from each state to indirectly elect the President and Vice President

popular sovereignty   a principle in which the people are the only source of government power

limited government   a principle stating that the government has only as much authority as the people give it and, therefore, its power is limited

separation of powers   a principle that divides power among the executive, legislative, and judicial branches of government

checks and balances   a system in which each branch of the government has the power to monitor and limit the actions of the other two

Name _____ Class _____ Date _____

Topic 4 Review Questions
ESTABLISHING THE NEW NATION

Answer the questions below using the information in the Lesson Summaries on the previous pages.

Lesson 1: The Articles of Confederation

1. What was one cause of tension between the United States and Britain?

2. **Identify Main Ideas** Identify three provisions of the Articles of Confederation that weakened the new U.S. government.

Lesson 2: The Constitutional Convention

3. In 1787, what two powers did most Americans believe Congress should have?

4. **Identify Supporting Details** List details of both the Virginia Plan and the New Jersey Plan.

Lesson 3: The Enduring Constitution

5. Why did the Federalists want the new Constitution to be ratified?

6. **Identify Main Ideas** How did the ratified Constitution including the first ten amendments reflect the views of both Federalists and Antifederalists?

Name _____ Class _____ Date _____

TOPIC 5
Note Taking Study Guide
THE EARLY REPUBLIC

Focus Question: What events, inventions, and ideas helped the United States expand in its early years?

As you read, focus on the factors that contributed to U.S. expansion from the late 1700s through the age of Jackson. Identify events, innovations, and ideas that helped the country grow and allowed different parts of the country to connect. Briefly explain the significance of each event or idea.

[Web diagram with central circle labeled "U.S. Growth and Expansion" connected to eight empty surrounding circles]

Name _____ Class _____ Date _____

TOPIC 5
LESSON 1

Lesson Summary
THE NEW GOVERNMENT FINDS ITS WAY

MODIFIED CORNELL NOTES

In 1789, the new electoral college unanimously elected George Washington as President of the United States. John Adams became Vice President. The **administration** began with only Washington, Adams, and some clerks. Besides the newly elected Congress, there were no other federal officers. After taking office, Washington began setting important **precedents**, or acts that become traditions to be followed. One precedent was the formation of a Cabinet, or the group of federal leaders who headed the major departments of the executive branch and served as advisers to the President. Congress passed the Judiciary Act, which set up the judicial branch.

As Secretary of the Treasury, Alexander Hamilton was given the task of paying off the nation's immense debts. Hamilton meant to pay the national debt by selling government bonds. He also called for high **tariffs** to raise revenue for the federal government. Hamilton thought his system would promote the accumulation of wealth needed for commercial and industrial growth.

Thomas Jefferson and James Madison led the opposition to Hamilton's plan, framing it in terms of how the Constitution should be interpreted. Hamilton's broad interpretation, or **loose construction**, relied on the Constitution's "implied powers" and its clauses empowering Congress to enact laws for the "general welfare." Jefferson and Madison favored a **strict construction**, or limiting the federal government to powers explicitly granted by the Constitution.

In 1794, the excise tax on whiskey led to rebellion. Farmers resisted the whiskey tax by attacking tax collectors. Washington and Hamilton demonstrated the new power of the nation by sending militia to suppress the Whiskey Rebellion.

(Continues on the next page.)

Lesson Vocabulary

administration staff of the executive branch

precedent an act or statement that becomes an example, rule, or tradition to be followed

tariff a tax on imported goods

loose construction a belief that the government has any power not forbidden by the Constitution

strict construction a belief that the government is limited to powers clearly stated in the Constitution

Name _____ Class _____ Date _____

Topic 5, Lesson 1

Lesson Summary
THE NEW GOVERNMENT FINDS ITS WAY (continued)

MODIFIED CORNELL NOTES

In the aftermath of the Whiskey Rebellion, the growing division in American politics became more apparent. The federal government, headed by Washington and Hamilton, sought to secure its power and authority. Meanwhile the opposition, led by Madison and Jefferson, grew stronger. The authors of the Constitution wanted to avoid organized **political parties**. However, practical politics resulted in the formation of two parties: the Federalists, led by Hamilton and John Adams, and the Democratic Republicans, led by Jefferson.

On the western frontier, the British helped American Indians resist U.S. expansion. Federal troops defeated an alliance of American Indian nations at the Battle of Fallen Timbers, opening up the Northwest Territory to settlement. The young nation also had to deal with foreign affairs. In 1789 a revolution in France raised political tensions in the United States, with Federalists condemning the French revolutionaries and Democratic Republicans supporting them. In the 1790s, war between Britain and France made it difficult for the United States to stay neutral, and Britain's practice of seizing American ships trading with French colonies led to another crisis. To avoid war with Britain, Chief Justice John Jay negotiated the Jay Treaty of 1794. The British gave up their forts on American soil but Americans had to repay prewar debts to the British. A year later, Pinckney's Treaty with Spain gave Americans free shipping rights on the Mississippi River and established the northern boundary of Spanish Florida. With these national and international successes, Washington decided not to run again for President and retired to his plantation. In his farewell address, he urged the nation to avoid "entangling alliances" that might lead to overseas wars.

In the 1796 presidential election, the Federalist candidate, John Adams, defeated Thomas Jefferson. Foreign affairs troubled Adams's administration, as the French began seizing American merchant ships. Negotiations in Paris ended abruptly when three French officials demanded bribes. Congress authorized a small navy to combat the French, but this meant raising unpopular taxes on Americans. In 1798 the Federalists passed the controversial Alien and Sedition Acts, which allowed the President to arrest and deport non-citizens who criticized the federal government. The acts effectively silenced dissent, as they made it a crime for citizens to criticize the federal government. In angry response, Jefferson and Madison wrote the Virginia and Kentucky resolutions, declaring the Sedition Act unconstitutional. Faced with mounting opposition to his policies, Adams sent diplomats to France to seek peace, but those moves in turn angered the Federalists, and Adams lost the presidential election of 1800 to Thomas Jefferson. In 1804 the Constitution was amended to require electors to vote separately for President and Vice President. In that same year, Vice President Aaron Burr killed his longtime rival Alexander Hamilton in a duel.

Lesson Vocabulary

political party a organization of people that seeks to win elections and hold public office in order to shape government policy

Name _____ Class _____ Date _____

TOPIC 5 LESSON 2
Lesson Summary
JEFFERSON AS PRESIDENT

MODIFIED CORNELL NOTES

The Jefferson administration set out to do things differently. Jefferson recognized the popularity of a common style. Many saw his election as a "revolution." Jefferson encouraged Congress to abandon the Alien and Sedition Acts, as well as the hated federal taxes. He cut the national debt. He made major cuts in the military and streamlined the government's **bureaucracy**, or the departments and workers that make up the government.

When Jefferson became President in 1801, John Marshall became the Chief Justice. Marshall's appointment had a major impact. His Supreme Court claimed the power to review the acts of Congress and the President to determine whether they were constitutional. This power is known as **judicial review**. The case of *Marbury v. Madison* established the power of judicial review.

In 1803, the Louisiana Purchase from France nearly doubled the size of the United States. Beginning in 1804, Jefferson sent Meriwether Lewis and William Clark to explore the new territory, in what became known as the Lewis and Clark Expedition.

While Jefferson succeeded in his plans to expand to the west, he also needed to solidify the position of the United States as an international power. The Barbary States of North Africa were seizing Americans ships and sailors in the Mediterranean Sea. Jefferson had paid protection money to the Barbary States, but when the price increased, Jefferson blockaded the port of Tripoli, winning a favorable peace in the Barbary War in 1805.

American farmers expanded, selling their **surplus** produce in overseas markets. From 1793 to 1807, war in Europe aided this goal.

Engaged in a tough war and desperately needing sailors, Britain relied on **impressment**, or taking American sailors from their ships and forcing them to be British sailors. As an alternative to war in 1807, Jefferson persuaded Congress to declare an embargo, or suspending trade by ordering American ships to stay in port. The British found other markets, while the **embargo** hurt American merchants, sailors, and farmers. Exploiting voter anger, the Federalists staged a political comeback in the northern states.

Lesson Vocabulary

bureaucracy a group of departments and officials that make up an organization, such as a government

judicial review the power of the Supreme Court to decide whether the acts of a president or laws passed by Congress are constitutional

surplus more than is needed

impressment a policy of seizing people or property for military or public service

embargo an official ban or restriction on trade

Name _____ Class _____ Date _____

Topic 5 Lesson 3

Lesson Summary
THE WAR OF 1812

MODIFIED CORNELL NOTES

On the western frontier, American Indian resistance was increasing. The warrior Tecumseh wanted to unite the Indian nations in armed resistance against American expansion. William Henry Harrison led troops in the Battle of Tippecanoe. This battle ended in stalemate, but as a result of it, the American Indian movement lost **momentum**.

In 1811, some young aggressive politicians known as the War Hawks pushed for war against Britain. Angry about the continued impressments of American sailors and British support for American Indians, the War Hawks insisted that invading British-held Canada would drive the British out of North America. In the War of 1812, the United States went to war with Britain.

The United States' attempts to invade Canada were unsuccessful. The small British and American Indian forces repeatedly defeated the poorly trained U.S. army and state militias. To the surprise of many Americans, the small American navy performed well, capturing four British ships during 1812.

In 1814, British forces invaded the United States in Maine, New York, Maryland, Washington, D.C., and New Orleans. Except for the occupation of Maine, the British attacks ended in defeat. The British did capture the national capital and burned the White House and the Capitol. Francis Scott Key celebrated the American victory at Fort McHenry in a poem called "The Star-Spangled Banner". The Americans won their greatest victory at the Battle of New Orleans under Andrew Jackson. The victory helped **bolster** American pride.

The Americans had failed to conquer Canada, while the British had failed in their American invasions. In the Treaty of Ghent, both sides agreed to prewar boundaries.

The outcome of the war discredited the Federalists, who looked weak for opposing a war that became popular once it was over. By 1820, the Federalist Party was dead.

Events during the War of 1812 ended most American Indian resistance to American expansion for the time being. The Treaty of Ghent forced the British to give up their forts in America, opening the way to American expansion.

Lesson Vocabulary

momentum   force or speed of motion
bolster   to improve or support

Copyright © by Pearson Education, Inc., or its affiliates. All Rights Reserved.

TOPIC 5 LESSON 4

Lesson Summary
THE BEGINNING OF THE INDUSTRIAL REVOLUTION

MODIFIED CORNELL NOTES

In the early 1800s, the transportation revolution changed the economy of the United States. As new methods of transportation developed, the cost of moving goods dropped and businesses grew.

Some states chartered companies to operate **turnpikes**—roads for which users had to pay a toll. However, most of these roads did not succeed in increasing the speed of travel. The country's first major road was the National Road, which was funded by the federal government.

Steamboats provided the first major advance in transportation. This invention allowed goods and people to be carried upstream much faster. The construction of canals also made water transportation more efficient. Most canals were built by the government. The Erie Canal connected Lake Erie to New York City. Later, the growth of railroads allowed vast new areas to gain **access** to new markets.

New technology was also changing manufacturing in a transformation that came to be known as the Industrial Revolution. Entrepreneurs began this revolution by developing machines to perform the work that had once been done by hand. These machines were powered by steam or moving water.

Samuel Slater, a skilled English worker, moved to America and built the nation's first water-powered textile mill in 1793. A flowing river provided power for the mill's machinery to make cotton thread. In 1813, Boston merchant Francis Cabot Lowell built a fully operational mill that could make all parts of cloth, instead of just thread. The growth of factories like these changed the working lives of thousands of people. Machines increased the pace of work and divided labor into many small tasks that required less skill. The invention of **interchangeable parts**, identical **components** that could be used in place of one another, also improved manufacturing efficiency. Eli Whitney is credited with this invention.

Other areas of American life were also changed by technology. Samuel F.B. Morse invented the electric telegraph in 1837, which made communication much faster. Food production also greatly increased when new farming methods were developed.

Lesson Vocabulary

turnpike   a road that requires users to pay a toll

access   the means of getting or acquiring

interchangeable parts   identical components that can be used in place of one another

component   part; one of the parts of a whole

Name _____ Class _____ Date _____

Topic 5 Lesson 5

Lesson Summary
DIFFERENCES BETWEEN NORTH AND SOUTH GROW

MODIFIED CORNELL NOTES

In the early 1800s, the North became more industrialized while the South became mostly agricultural. Industrialization spread across the North for several reasons. The Tariff of 1816 was a protective tariff that helped American manufacturers by increasing the cost of imported goods, which encouraged Americans to buy products made in the United States. Factories also appeared in the North because there was greater access to **capital**, or the money needed to buy equipment and factories. In the South, capital was tied up in land and slaves.

Another reason for industrialization was the abundance of labor. Millions of immigrants came to the United States during this period. Most of them were poor and went to work in northeastern cities. Often these immigrants were treated poorly. Many Protestant workers resented the competition from poor, Catholic immigrants. Some politicians, called **nativists**, campaigned for laws to discourage immigration or to deny political rights to newcomers.

Industrialization changed how people worked. New jobs required less skill, and skilled workers saw their wages go down. Some workers formed **labor unions**—groups of workers who unite to seek mutual goals. One tactic of labor unions was to go on strike, hoping to force employers to pay higher wages.

Many Americans benefited from new office jobs that were created during industrialization. These well-paid workers made up a new social and economic class—a middle class. In the South, a boom in agriculture was caused by the **cotton gin**, western expansion, and industrialization in the North. The cotton gin was an invention that made cotton cultivation easier and more profitable. More and more farmers began to grow cotton, including those who lived in new territories to the west. Demand for cotton continued to increase from factories in the North and in Europe.

The culture of the South was affected by its agriculture. The cotton boom was an incentive for farmers to acquire more slaves. Southerners claimed that slavery was good for society, and they had a sense of racial superiority. Education was not a high priority, so illiteracy was higher in the South than it was in the North.

Lesson Vocabulary

capital   money or wealth used to invest in business or enterprise

nativist   a person who favors native-born inhabitants over immigrants

labor union   an organization of workers

cotton gin   a machine invented in 1793 to separate the cotton fiber from its hard shell

Name _____ Class _____ Date _____

TOPIC 5 LESSON 6

Lesson Summary
NATIONALISM INFLUENCES POLICIES

MODIFIED CORNELL NOTES

After the War of 1812, **nationalism** swept the country. This was a feeling of glorification and promotion of the nation.

When Congress passed tariffs, it was expressing nationalism by using federal power to help industrialists and their workers. Henry Clay was one of the leading **advocates** of this new economic nationalism. He supported a large federal program called the American System for building new roads and canals to connect regions and help business.

The Supreme Court also took measures to strengthen the federal government. In several rulings, it interpreted the Constitution in a way that gave wide powers, such as the principle that federal law was superior to state law, to the government.

Nationalism also affected art and literature. Artists celebrated the nation's beautiful landscape, and novelists expressed pride in the nation's immense potential.

During this period of time, the economy experienced periodic shocks called panics, the results of "busts" in a "boom-and-bust" cycle that is common in capitalism.

The effects of nationalism also appeared in the government's foreign policy. John Quincy Adams, the Secretary of State under James Monroe, used the First Seminole War to expand the nation. In this war, American soldiers fought the Seminoles in Florida, which was a part of Spain. General Andrew Jackson led troops into Florida and captured some Spanish forts, making it clear that Spanish control over Florida was very weak. Adams pressured Spain to sell Florida to the United States as part of the Adams-Onís Treaty. The treaty also ended Spanish claims to the territory of Oregon.

Adams also formulated the Monroe Doctrine. This statement of policy, named for President Monroe, declared that European powers should stay out of the Western Hemisphere. The doctrine showed the nation's growing sense of its own importance.

Despite strong feelings of nationalism, there were still differences between regions in the United States. In 1820, the Missouri Compromise addressed the heated debate over slavery. The act maintained the balance of slave and free states. The compromise was only a temporary solution, however.

Lesson Vocabulary

nationalism   loyalty and devotion to one's nation
advocate   person who supports or urges for something

Name _____ Class _____ Date _____

TOPIC 5 LESSON 7
Lesson Summary
JACKSONIAN DEMOCRACY

MODIFIED CORNELL NOTES

In the election of 1824, the four candidates who ran for President were from the Democratic Republican Party, the only major political party at the time. War hero Andrew Jackson enjoyed wide public support. However, the election was so close that the House of Representatives had to declare the winner. Jackson was upset over losing and spent the next four years campaigning to win the presidency in 1828.

Jackson traveled the country, hoping to **exploit** the increasingly democratic character of national politics. In the 1824 presidential election, some states chose electors based on popular votes, a shift from earlier elections in which state legislatures chose the electors. A key Jackson aide was New York's Martin Van Buren. Van Buren worked behind the scenes to build support for Jackson.

Andrew Jackson became the symbol of this expanded democracy. Historians refer to the movement as Jacksonian Democracy. In public, Jackson celebrated majority rule and the dignity of common people. He also had an appealing personal story. He was born in a log cabin and orphaned as a boy. Jackson won the election of 1828 easily. His party was now called the Democratic Party, and it promised a return to strong states and a weak federal government.

The party created a new, more disciplined and professional organizational structure. It rewarded loyal supporters with government jobs, a practice called the **spoils system** by critics.

One of Jackson's highest priorities was removing the 60,000 American Indians living in the South. Southern whites wanted the land for themselves, and they got their wish with the Indian Removal Act of 1830. This act sought to exchange Indian lands for new lands in Indian Territory.

Although most Indians agreed to leave their homelands, some did not. U.S. soldiers forced 16,000 Cherokees to walk to their new home in modern-day Oklahoma. This forced march came to be called the Trail of Tears because at least 4,000 Cherokees died of disease, exposure, and hunger. Some Seminoles violently resisted the government's demands by fighting the Second Seminole War.

(Continues on the next page.)

Lesson Vocabulary

exploit   to take advantage of; utilize

spoils system   the practice of the political party in power giving jobs and appointments to its supporters, rather than to people based on their qualifications

Name _____ Class _____ Date _____

TOPIC 5 LESSON 7

Lesson Summary
JACKSONIAN DEMOCRACY (continued)

MODIFIED CORNELL NOTES

The presidency of Andrew Jackson featured a number of conflicts. In 1828, Congress adopted a high tariff that became known as the Tariff of Abominations. In general, tariffs were favored by the North and disliked by the South. The fact that President Adams signed this tariff helped to bring about his defeat in 1828. Although Jackson was against tariffs, he did not remove them as President.

When the tariff was not abolished, Vice President John C. Calhoun got upset. Calhoun was from South Carolina and strongly against tariffs. He argued for **nullification**, the idea that states could nullify, or void, any federal law they deemed unconstitutional.

Even though Jackson did not support tariffs, he signed a new one into law. In 1833, South Carolina took action by nullifying the protective tariff and prohibiting the collection of tariff duties. The state also threatened to secede from the Union.

Jackson supported states' rights and low tariffs, but he rejected nullification and secession. He felt the Union must be perpetual and states must honor federal law. Congress gave Jackson the authority to use troops to enforce federal law in South Carolina. At the same time, Congress also reduced the tariff. This reduced South Carolina's anger, and the state ended its policy of nullification.

Jackson faced another conflict over the national bank. The Second Bank of the United States had been created by Congress in 1816. Jackson and his supporters opposed the Bank and argued that it mostly benefited the rich. However, the Bank had many supporters in Congress, and in 1832, they voted to renew the Bank's charter. Jackson vetoed the bill, stating that the bank was unconstitutional and did not benefit the public.

Anger over Jackson's veto led to the creation of the political party known as the Whigs. The Whigs wanted a strong federal government to manage the economy. When the economy soured after Jackson's replacement Martin Van Buren served as President, the Whigs managed to get their candidate, William Henry Harrison, elected President. However, he died shortly after taking office, and his replacement rejected Whig policies.

Lesson Vocabulary

nullification   concept in which states could nullify, or void, any federal law they deemed unconstitutional

Name _____ Class _____ Date _____

TOPIC 5 — Review Questions
THE EARLY REPUBLIC

Answer the questions below using the information in the Lesson Summaries on the previous pages.

Lesson 1: The New Government Finds Its Way

1. What was the purpose of the Cabinet?
_____
_____

2. Summarize Summarize how the two-party system emerged in the new nation.
_____
_____
_____

Lesson 2: Jefferson as President

3. What was the importance of the Louisiana Purchase?
_____
_____

4. Identify Main Ideas Identify three accomplishments of Jefferson's presidency.
_____
_____
_____

Lesson 3: The War of 1812

5. Recognize Sequence Identify the causes of the War of 1812.
_____
_____
_____

6. Name two results of the War of 1812 that benefited the United States.
_____
_____
_____

Lesson 4: The Beginning of the Industrial Revolution

7. How was the production of goods affected by the Industrial Revolution?
_____
_____

8. Identify Causes and Effects Provide at least two effects of the transportation revolution and industrialization.
_____
_____

Name _____ Class _____ Date _____

TOPIC 5 Review Questions
THE EARLY REPUBLIC (continued)

Lesson 5: Differences Between North and South Grow

9. **Compare and Contrast** Describe the similarities and differences between the new American immigrants and Protestant workers.
_____
_____

10. What factors caused a boom in southern agriculture?
_____
_____

Lesson 6: Nationalism Influences Politics

11. How did the American System express nationalism?
_____
_____

12. **Understand Effects** The capture of some Spanish forts by General Andrew Jackson led to what effect?
_____
_____

Lesson 7: Jacksonian Democracy

13. Why was Jacksonian Democracy popular with the public?
_____
_____

14. **Understand Effects** Describe the effects resulting from Jackson's desire to remove the 60,000 American Indians living in the South.
_____
_____

Name _____ Class _____ Date _____

TOPIC 6
Note Taking Study Guide
RESHAPING AMERICA IN THE EARLY 1800S

Focus Question: What reform movements worked for change in nineteenth-century America? What effects did these movements have?

As you read, focus on the reform movements that worked for change in the early 1800s. Identify each movement. Then record the effects or accomplishments their work had achieved by the mid-1800s.

Reform Movements

Copyright © by Pearson Education, Inc., or its affiliates. All Rights Reserved.

Name _____ Class _____ Date _____

TOPIC 6 LESSON 1
Lesson Summary
MOVING WEST

MODIFIED CORNELL NOTES

In the 1600s and 1700s, Spanish settlers spread into New Mexico, Texas, and California, where they set up ranches, missions, and presidios. However, these areas remained sparsely populated. Lacking colonists, the Spanish leaders in California sought to convert Indians to Christianity. Franciscan priests led by Father Junípero Serra set up a string of missions that became more successful than those in Texas or New Mexico. However, conflicts between the Spanish and American Indian groups remained a problem.

In 1821, a revolution ended Spanish rule in Mexico. The U.S. government recognized Mexico's independence. However, **expansionists** quickly began to covet the territories of northern Mexico. These Americans thought that the Mexican government and economy were weak and that the territory should belong to the United States. This idea, known as Manifest Destiny, claimed that it was God's plan for the United States to own most or all of North America.

Mexican independence spurred U.S. trade with Mexico, allowing merchants to establish an active trading route along the Santa Fe Trail. This trade benefited Mexico, but the U.S. traders and settlers would come to threaten the security of Mexico's border.

Adventurous men known as Mountain Men also traveled west. They worked as fur trappers, explored the Rocky Mountains, and established new trails, which settlers used to travel westward. By the 1840s, large wagon trains were taking settlers west in great numbers. Commencing in springtime in Missouri, the demanding journey covered nearly 2,000 miles and took about five months to complete. Despite the hardships of the journey, settlers **persevered**. One popular trail became known as the Oregon Trail.

The religious group called the Mormons had a different reason than most for moving west. They were fleeing religious persecution. Their leader, Brigham Young, led migrants west to establish a colony on the eastern shore of the Great Salt Lake.

Most settlers were left alone by American Indians during their move west. However, the federal government still sought to ensure their safety. The 1851 Treaty of Fort Laramie bound the Indians to territories away from the major trails.

Lesson Vocabulary

expansionist a person who favors expanding the territory or influence of a country

persevere to do something despite its difficulty

Name _____ Class _____ Date _____

TOPIC 6 LESSON 2
Lesson Summary
TEXAS AND THE MEXICAN-AMERICAN WAR

MODIFIED CORNELL NOTES

In 1821, only a few thousand Hispanics, known as Tejanos, lived in Texas. To develop the territory, Mexico invited Americans to settle there. In return for cheap land grants, Americans had to agree to become Mexican citizens, to become Roman Catholics, and to accept the Mexican constitution banning slavery.

Led by Stephen F. Austin, these settlers came in large numbers. By 1835, American settlers outnumbered Tejanos by six to one. However, tension was growing between the settlers and the Mexican government. The settlers were **reluctant** to honor the agreement they had made with Mexico when they accepted the land grants. They were also unhappy with Mexico's ruthless leader, Antonio López de Santa Anna. The settlers wanted greater **autonomy**, or more control over their own affairs. In 1835, the Texans rebelled against the Mexican government. The rebels declared independence and called their new nation the Lone Star Republic.

Santa Anna led his army north to attack the Texans. At the Alamo, a former mission in San Antonio, Mexican troops slaughtered the Texans. The bloody defeat motivated the Texans to fight even harder. Sam Houston led the Texan army in a surprise attack on Santa Anna's army. Houston's men won, and Santa Anna was forced to sign a treaty recognizing Texan independence.

The Mexican government refused to honor the treaty. A border war persisted for the next decade. When the U.S. Congress voted to annex Texas as a state in 1845, Mexico was outraged. President James K. Polk supported the annexation.

Polk won the election by supporting the annexation of Texas and Oregon. Americans who opposed Polk feared that he planned to annex the Mexican provinces **adjacent** to Texas, including New Mexico and California. Polk pushed the nation closer to war by ordering U.S. troops into the contested borderlands in Texas. General Zachary Taylor led these troops. In May 1846, a border clash between U.S. and Mexican troops in which Americans were killed led Polk to declare war on Mexico.

The United States had many advantages, including its size, wealth, and larger population. In 1847, General Winfield Scott captured Mexico City. America had won a sweeping victory over Mexico.

Lesson Vocabulary

reluctant unwilling; marked by mental hesitation or reservations
autonomy the independent control of one's own affairs
adjacent neighboring; nearby

Name _____ Class _____ Date _____

Topic 6 Lesson 3

Lesson Summary
AMERICA ACHIEVES MANIFEST DESTINY

MODIFIED CORNELL NOTES

In February 1848, the defeated Mexicans made peace with the United States in the Treaty of Guadalupe Hidalgo. Mexico was forced to give up the northern third of their country. In 1853, the Untied States gained territory in southern Arizona and New Mexico from Mexico in the Gadsden Purchase. The new lands **comprised** present-day New Mexico, California, Nevada, Utah, Arizona, and half of Colorado.

The Mexican-American War had many far-reaching effects. The new territories made the fight over slavery even more heated. Whigs proposed the Wilmot Proviso, a law that would have prohibited slavery in the new territories. Congress broke into northern and southern groups, and major political parties were divided. The Wilmot Proviso never passed, but it brought the slavery issue to the forefront and weakened the two major parties.

In 1848, workers at a sawmill on the West Coast discovered gold. The discovery set off the California Gold Rush. This mass migration brought tens of thousands of people west. About half of these **forty-niners** traveled by land, and another half went by sea. Forty-niners also came from South America and China. In just five years, California's population jumped by more than 200,000 people. Most of these miners had a difficult, violent life. They worked hard, earned little, and suffered from disease and terrible living conditions.

At first, most miners used **placer mining**, in which each miner tried to find gold in rivers and streams and along the banks with little equipment. Over time, however, better equipment was used. **Hydraulic mining**, which employed jets of water to erode gravel hills, and "hard rock mining" were both more effective, but they also damaged the environment more.

The rapid settlement of California had unforeseen consequences. American Indians were killed and terrorized by the thousands. Many Mexican Americans lost their land and their rights. California also caused a problem when it applied for statehood. At that time, the number of slave and free states was equal. However, if California became a free state, it would tip the balance. Northern and southern congressmen debated slavery yet again.

Lesson Vocabulary

comprised made up of

forty-niner a miner who went to California after the discovery of gold in 1848

placer mining the use of metal pans, picks, and shovels to harvest gold from the banks and bottoms of rivers and streams

hydraulic mining the use of water to erode gravel hills into long sluices to catch any gold

MODIFIED CORNELL NOTES

TOPIC 6 LESSON 4

Lesson Summary
A RELIGIOUS AWAKENING SPARKS REFORM

In the early 1700s, Americans experienced a burst of religious energy known as the Great Awakening. Another revival of religious feeling, the Second Great Awakening, swept the country in the early 1800s. Protestant preachers known as **revivalists** taught that religion was vital to the nation.

This excitement about religion started in Kentucky and spread across the nation. Revivalists such as Charles Grandison Finney taught listeners in large outdoor gatherings called "revivals." Finney gave passionate sermons that were emotionally moving. This **evangelical** style of preaching proved very successful in winning converts. African Americans were also part of this movement. They attended revivals and sometimes started their own churches.

Excitement about religion also led to the formation of two new religious groups. In 1830, Joseph Smith established the Church of Jesus Christ of Latter-day Saints. His followers were commonly called the Mormons. In New England, some members of Puritan churches broke away into a new group called the Unitarians. They believed that God was a single divine being instead of a "Trinity."

As Protestant believers grew in their enthusiasm and political power, some non-Protestants faced persecution. Mormons faced violence when their neighbors opposed their beliefs. Catholics and Jews faced **discrimination** in the early 1800s, too. In some places, Protestants rioted against Catholic worshippers. State constitutions, from New England to the South, barred Jews from holding public office. Americans often ostracized Jews.

Some groups took advantage of abundant land and established **utopian communities**. They hoped these settlements would be perfect worlds where all residents worked together. In New England, a group known as the Transcendentalists developed a new way to look at humanity, nature, and God. Writers like Ralph Waldo Emerson and Henry David Thoreau thought that people could transcend, or go beyond, their senses to learn about the world and to learn the truth about the universe.

(Continues on the next page.)

Lesson Vocabulary

revivalist a preacher who works to renew the importance of religion in American life

evangelical a style of worship meant to elicit powerful emotions to gain converts

discrimination unfair bias in the treatment of a particular group

utopian community separate settlement established with the goal of moral perfection

Name _____ Class _____ Date _____

TOPIC 6
LESSON 4

Lesson Summary
A RELIGIOUS AWAKENING SPARKS REFORM (continued)

MODIFIED CORNELL NOTES

In the early and middle 1800s, many Americans worked to reform American life and to help disadvantaged people. Reformers tackled problems in several areas of public life.

Many reformers thought that education in America was inadequate. Because there were no tax-supported schools that children were required to attend, most children did not receive a formal education. The **public school movement** tried to establish state-supported schools. Reformers thought that education would give Americans the **intellectual** tools needed to keep the nation strong. School reformers, such as Horace Mann, also tried to ensure that schools were funded and had good teachers. Over the next few decades, public schools became common nationwide. Many women, such as Catharine Beecher, played key roles in the school reform movement. Beecher helped establish schools for women.

Some reformers tried to help the mentally ill. Dorothea Dix discovered that many mentally ill patients were placed in prisons along with criminals. By encouraging her state and many others to build humane hospitals for the mentally ill, she promoted the creation of the first modern mental hospitals.

Dorothea Dix also collaborated with others to reform the prison system. The **penitentiary movement** sought to change prisons and make them less cruel. Due to the efforts of these reformers, prisoners were less isolated and received better treatment.

Some reformers blamed societal ills on the abuse of alcohol, believing it was the root cause of most crime, poverty, and family neglect. Reformers launched **the temperance movement** to end alcohol abuse. Temperance means drinking alcoholic beverages in moderation. Reformers warned the public that drinking alcohol led to many social problems.

The temperance movement only had real success when reformers, such as Neal Dow, won changes in the law. Dow became the mayor of Portland, Maine. He convinced Maine to pass a law restricting the sale of alcohol, setting a precedent that many other states chose to follow.

Lesson Vocabulary

public school movement   a movement aimed at providing greater educational opportunities through the establishment of tax-supported public schools

intellectual   related to the ability to understand difficult ideas

penitentiary movement   a movement aimed at structuring prisons so that prisoners would feel penitent for their crimes

temperance movement   a movement aimed at stopping alcohol abuse and the problems created by it

MODIFIED CORNELL NOTES

Topic 6, Lesson 5

Lesson Summary
THE ABOLITION MOVEMENT

In the early 1800s, around two million Africans and African Americans were held as slaves in the United States. Most of these men, women, and children labored all day at difficult tasks. They faced physical punishment if they did not do their work and were provided with barely enough food, clothing, and shelter.

Slaves tried to maintain some hope and dignity by relying on networks of family and friends and taking comfort in their religion, a mix of African and Christian beliefs. Other slaves resisted their masters by escaping or revolting. Denmark Vesey, a **freedman**, or former slave, planned a large slave revolt in 1822. His plan failed, but Nat Turner's revolt was more successful. Turner was a slave who led followers on a violent revolt that alarmed slaveholders.

Many northerners had objected to slavery for decades on moral grounds. Many of these Americans were part of the **abolition movement**, and they wanted slavery abolished, or ended. One leading abolitionist, William Lloyd Garrison, published an antislavery newspaper called *The Liberator*. Garrison tried to convince the public that slavery was morally wrong. He also created the American Anti-Slavery Society, whose 150,000 members worked across the nation to abolish slavery.

Another famous abolitionist was Frederick Douglass. This former slave was an effective lecturer against slavery and even served as an adviser to President Lincoln during the Civil War.

Most Americans still opposed abolishing slavery. Slaveholders argued that the southern economy would collapse without slavery. Some southerners claimed that Christianity supported slavery or that slaves could not survive without their masters. They felt that Africans were inferior and that their enslavement was historically **inevitable**. Many northerners opposed abolition, too. Some feared that African Americans would take their jobs.

Most white northerners did not like the controversy about slavery and did not want to discuss abolition. In 1836, southern politicians helped pass a Gag Rule in Congress. This law prohibited Congress from discussing abolition for many years.

Lesson Vocabulary

freedman a person who has been freed from slavery

abolition movement a nineteenth century movement that sought an end to slavery

inevitable impossible to prevent; unavoidable

Name _____ Class _____ Date _____

TOPIC 6 LESSON 6

Lesson Summary
WOMEN WORK FOR CHANGE

MODIFIED CORNELL NOTES

In the 1800s, American women's freedom and rights were sharply limited. Women were not allowed to have a visible role in public life, and they lacked many basic legal and economic rights. They could not own property, hold office, or vote, and very few received a formal education.

Some groups living in America, such as certain American Indians, had different traditions. Some cultures were **matrilineal**, meaning that inheritance of family names and property followed the female line in the family.

Many new opportunities for women came from the Second Great Awakening. Churches sponsored some reform groups, and many abolitionist groups were made up entirely of women. One of the most effective abolitionist lecturers was Sojourner Truth, a former slave. Women also found some opportunities by working outside of the home, which gave them a small degree of economic independence.

Many women compared their lack of rights to slavery. Despite some advances, there had been virtually no progress in women's rights. Reformers in the **women's movement** across the country began to call for greater rights.

Most women reformers did not seek full equality. However, Lucretia Mott and Elizabeth Cady Stanton did. These two abolitionists organized the nation's first Women's Rights Convention. Often called the Seneca Falls Convention, the meeting attracted hundreds of men and women. The meeting inspired many women, including Amelia Bloomer, who went on to publish a newspaper that advocated equality for women.

By the middle of the 1800s, American women had laid the foundation for a future in which equality seemed like a real possibility. For example, in 1848, New York passed the Married Women's Property Act. This law guaranteed many property rights for women. Over time, the women's movement narrowed its focus to one goal: **suffrage**, or the right to vote.

Lesson Vocabulary

matrilineal when inheritance is passed down through the female side of the family

women's movement a movement beginning in the mid-1800s in the United States that sought greater rights and opportunities for women

suffrage the right to vote

Copyright © by Pearson Education, Inc., or its affiliates. All Rights Reserved.

Name _____ Class _____ Date _____

TOPIC 6: Review Questions
RESHAPING AMERICA IN THE EARLY 1800S

Answer the questions below, using the information in the Lesson Summaries on the previous pages.

Lesson 1: Moving West

1. What did expansionists want to acquire?
   _____
   _____

2. **Identify Main Ideas** What was the most common method for settlers to move westward?
   _____
   _____

Lesson 2: Texas and the Mexican-American War

3. How did Texas come to be dominated by American settlers?
   _____
   _____

4. **Recognize Sequence** After Congress voted to annex Texas in 1845, what step led the United States closer to war with Mexico?
   _____
   _____

Lesson 3: America Achieves Manifest Destiny

5. Why was the Wilmot Proviso controversial?
   _____
   _____

6. **Understand Effects** What unforeseen consequences occurred during the settlement of California?
   _____
   _____

Lesson 4: A Religious Awakening Sparks Reform

7. **Identify Main Ideas** How did the revivalists win so many converts?
   _____
   _____

8. **Understand Effects** Provide an example of a reform that resulted from a reform movement.
   _____
   _____

Name _____ Class _____ Date _____

TOPIC 6 — Review Questions
RESHAPING AMERICA IN THE EARLY 1800S (continued)

Lesson 5: The Abolition Movement

9. List two ways that some enslaved people resisted their masters.
_____
_____

10. **Summarize** How did abolitionists and slaveholders differ in their views about slavery?
_____
_____

Lesson 6: Women Work for Change

11. What were some of the limits American women faced in the 1800s?
_____
_____

12. **Identify Causes and Effects** List at least two effects of the women's movement.
_____
_____

Copyright © by Pearson Education, Inc., or its affiliates. All Rights Reserved.

Name _____ Class _____ Date _____

Note Taking Study Guide
TOPIC 7 — SECTIONAL DIVISIONS AND THE CIVIL WAR

Focus Question: What events, developments, and conflicts helped cause the Civil War? What were the social, economic, and political effects of the war?

As you read, focus on the causes and effects of the Civil War. Record events, changes, and conflicts in the 1800s that helped lead to the beginning of war in 1861. Then note social, political, and economic changes that happened as a result of the war. A few bullet points have been provided, but you will need to add more.

Causes
-
-

↓ ↓

CIVIL WAR

↓ ↓

Effects
-
-

Name _____ Class _____ Date _____

Topic 7 Lesson 1
Lesson Summary
SLAVERY DIVIDES THE NATION

MODIFIED CORNELL NOTES

After the American Revolution, the North and the South developed different ways of life. The North developed busy cities, embraced technology and industry, and built factories. The South remained an agrarian, or agricultural, society. By the mid-nineteenth century, cotton cultivation and slavery had spread across the Deep South.

Americans faced this question: Should slavery be allowed in the new territories west of the Mississippi River? The balance of power between the North and the South—free and slave—depended on this decision. During the early days of the Mexican-American War, Pennsylvania congressman David Wilmot had proposed a law banning slavery from the lands won from Mexico. The northern-dominated House of Representatives approved the Wilmot Proviso, but the Senate voted it down.

Democrats and Whigs hoped to attract voters from all sides of the slavery debate. Members of the new Free-Soil Party wanted to limit slavery in the territories. Democrats and Whigs embraced the idea of **popular sovereignty**, a policy stating that the voters in a territory—not Congress—should decide whether to allow slavery. The 1848 presidential election was won by the Whig candidate, Zachary Taylor, a general and a hero of the Mexican-American War. He was also a slaveholder.

In 1848, gold was discovered in California, attracting people from all over the world. In 1849, the people of California drafted a constitution and asked that California be admitted to the Union as a free state. Because admitting California would tip the balance in favor of the free states, the southern states threatened to **secede**, or break away, from the Union. Senator Henry Clay put forth a number of compromise resolutions. Illinois Senator Stephen A. Douglas steered each **component** of Clay's plan through Congress separately. The Senate adopted legislation based on Clay's proposals, known as the Compromise of 1850. California was admitted as a free state, and the policy of popular sovereignty was applied to the territory acquired from Mexico. In addition, a new Fugitive Slave Act required that private citizens help apprehend runaway slaves. Though the Compromise of 1850 restored calm for the moment, it carried the seeds of new crises to come.

(Continues on the next page.)

Lesson Vocabulary

popular sovereignty   a principle in which the people are the only source of government power; in the 1850s, the term referred to a proposed policy of letting voters in new states and territories decide the question of whether to allow slavery

secede   to withdraw formally from a membership in a group or an organization

component   piece or element

Copyright © by Pearson Education, Inc., or its affiliates. All Rights Reserved.

Name _____ Class _____ Date _____

TOPIC 7 LESSON 1
Lesson Summary
SLAVERY DIVIDES THE NATION (continued)

MODIFIED CORNELL NOTES

The new Fugitive Slave Act, which required citizens to catch and return runaway slaves, enraged many northerners. Some northern states passed **personal liberty laws**, which nullified the Fugitive Slave Act. They also allowed the state to arrest slave catchers for kidnapping. Northern white bystanders refused to **intervene** to help slave hunters. A network known as the Underground Railroad helped runaway slaves escape to the North or to Canada. One of its most courageous conductors was former slave Harriet Tubman. She was known as "Black Moses" for leading her people out of bondage. In 1852, Harriet Beecher Stowe published the novel *Uncle Tom's Cabin*, a powerful condemnation of slavery.

Lesson Vocabulary

personal liberty laws   laws enacted by northern states to counteract the Fugitive Slave Act by granting rights to escaped slaves and free blacks

intervene   to get involved in a situation

Name _____ Class _____ Date _____

TOPIC 7 LESSON 2
Lesson Summary
VIOLENCE ESCALATES

MODIFIED CORNELL NOTES

The repeated attempts of Congress to resolve the question of slavery resulted in a jumble of contradictory policies. In 1854, Senator Douglas introduced a bill to set up a government in the Nebraska Territory. Under pressure from the South, Douglas amended the bill to divide the region into two territories, Kansas and Nebraska. Each territory would be organized according to popular sovereignty. The Kansas-Nebraska Act nullified the Missouri Compromise, allowing slavery to spread to areas that had been free for more than 30 years.

Most of the people who came to the new Kansas Territory were farmers looking for land. However, Kansas also attracted settlers with political motives. By 1855, a proslavery government near the Missouri border developed a proslavery constitution. Free-state advocates set up an antislavery government in Topeka. In 1856, the Topeka government petitioned Congress for statehood. On May 21, 1856, a proslavery group raided the antislavery town of Lawrence, Kansas. The abolitionist John Brown quickly retaliated. With his sons and a few friends, Brown executed five proslavery settlers. Throughout the fall of 1856, violent outbreaks occurred in various locales around Lawrence, leading reporters to characterize the situation as "Bleeding Kansas." It became clear that popular sovereignty was not the solution to the slavery question. Kansas was finally admitted as a free state in 1861.

Millard Fillmore was the last Whig President. He angered the South by supporting California's entry as a free state. Northerners left the party in large numbers because of his support for the Fugitive Slave Act and popular sovereignty. By the mid-1800s, increasing immigration was changing the country. An anti-immigrant movement developed. Dubbed the "Know-Nothings" because its members pretended to know nothing when questioned about their organization, the group grew rapidly. By 1855, they had formed the American Party. However, the new party soon divided over the issue of slavery in the western territories. Antislavery zeal gave rise to the new Republican Party in 1854, which grew rapidly in the North.

In the 1856 presidential election, the Republican candidate made a strong showing. However, Democrat James Buchanan won the election, supported by the large majority of southerners. Then, in 1857, the Supreme Court ruled in the case of a Missouri slave, Dred Scott, who had sued for his freedom. The court, under Chief Justice Roger B. Taney, ruled that slaves and their descendants were property, not citizens, and not entitled to sue in the courts. It also ruled that the Missouri Compromise was unconstitutional because it was illegal for Congress to **deprive** an owner of property—in this case, a slave—without due process of law.

(Continues on the next page.)

Lesson Vocabulary

deprive   to take away something important

Name _____ Class _____ Date _____

TOPIC 7 LESSON 2

Lesson Summary
VIOLENCE ESCALATES (continued)

MODIFIED CORNELL NOTES

In 1850, a series of debates between two candidates for an Illinois Senate seat attracted attention. Republican Abraham Lincoln opposed the Kansas-Nebraska Act and its **implicit** support for the expansion of slavery. His rival was Stephen A. Douglas, who promoted popular sovereignty as a solution to regional tensions. Douglas won the election by a slim margin.

Both men believed that the slavery issue had to be resolved within the law. Abolitionist John Brown felt no such constraints. He believed he was God's angel avenging the evil of slavery. He mounted an armed assault on slavery. In the fall of 1859, Brown and his followers set out to seize the federal arsenal in Harpers Ferry, Virginia. Brown hoped local slaves would join a revolution to destroy slavery. The effort failed. Some of the rebels were killed and some escaped. Brown's attack deepened the division between the North and the South.

Lesson Vocabulary

implicit   unspoken but understood

Name _____ Class _____ Date _____

Topic 7 Lesson 3: Lesson Summary
THE CIVIL WAR BEGINS

MODIFIED CORNELL NOTES

In 1860, anxiety ran high in both the North and the South as the presidential election approached. Mississippi Senator Jefferson Davis convinced Congress to restrict federal control over slavery in the territories and assert that the Constitution prohibited Congress or any state from interfering with slavery in states where it already existed. During the election of 1860, the Democrats split into two parties. Northern Democrats backed Stephen A. Douglas, who supported popular sovereignty, while southern Democrats nominated Vice President John C. Breckenridge, who wanted to expand slavery into the territories. The Republicans nominated Abraham Lincoln. Their platform called for an end to slavery in the territories. They **stipulated** that there should be no interference with slavery in the states. The split in the Democratic Party kept those candidates from getting enough votes to win the election. Instead, Lincoln won with 40 percent of the popular vote—but not a single southern electoral vote.

When Lincoln's election was confirmed, South Carolina seceded from the Union. In the next few weeks, six other states of the Deep South seceded. In February 1861, they established the Confederate States of America. The Confederate constitution stressed each state's independence and protected slavery. However, to win the support of Britain and France, it prohibited importing new slaves. The Confederacy chose Jefferson Davis as its President. In an attempt to compromise with the South, Kentucky Senator John Crittenden proposed a new constitutional amendment. If it had passed, the Crittenden Compromise would have allowed slavery in western territories south of the Missouri Compromise line. In his last weeks in office, President Buchanan told Congress that he had no authority to prevent secession.

In his inaugural address, Lincoln said that he did not intend to interfere with slavery in states where it existed. He intended to preserve the Union, but he would not start a war. When South Carolinians fired on Fort Sumter, a Union fort guarding the harbor at Charleston, President Lincoln called for 75,000 volunteers to fight against the Confederacy.

(Continues on the next page.)

Lesson Vocabulary

stipulate to specify or indicate

Name _____ **Class** _____ **Date** _____

Topic 7, Lesson 3 — Lesson Summary
THE CIVIL WAR BEGINS (continued)

MODIFIED CORNELL NOTES

The Union initially appeared to have the most advantages in the Civil War, due to its greater population and preparedness for war. In addition, the Union possessed most of the nation's mines, a large railroad network for moving troops and material, and a well-organized navy. The South had no navy at all, leaving it vulnerable to a naval **blockade** in which Union ships prevented merchant vessels from entering or leaving the South's few good ports, thereby crippling southern trade. The Confederacy had the psychological advantage: it was fighting for survival. The South also had a strong military tradition, strategic advantages, and fine leaders like Robert E. Lee.

The initial Union strategy was the Anaconda Plan. Union forces would blockade southern ports and take control of the Mississippi River, splitting the Confederacy in two. They faced the tricky question of keeping Missouri, Kentucky, Delaware, and Maryland in the Union. These **border states** allowed slavery but had not seceded. To reduce this threat, Lincoln insisted that his only goal was to save the Union. The Confederate strategy was to preserve its small armies while doing enough damage to **erode** the Union's will to fight. It also hoped for formal recognition from Britain and France.

In July 1861, Union and Confederate troops met at Bull Run, a creek near Manassas, Virginia. Confederate General Thomas J. Jackson earned the nickname Stonewall Jackson for his refusal to yield to Union armies. His troops sent the Union army scrambling back to Washington. After the Battle of Bull Run, Lincoln replaced the Union general with General George B. McClellan. Meanwhile, General Ulysses S. Grant pursued the Mississippi Valley wing of the Anaconda Plan. Union ships under David Farragut seized the port of New Orleans, Louisiana, at the mouth of the Mississippi. Both Farragut and Grant aimed for the Confederate stronghold of Vicksburg, Mississippi.

Major fighting in the East focused on Virginia. One notable naval battle was between two ironclad warships, the *Virginia* and the *Monitor*, in March 1862. It signaled the beginning of the end of wooden warships. Meanwhile, Lincoln had become impatient with McClellan's caution and replaced him.

Lesson Vocabulary

blockade a military tactic in which a navy prevents vessels from entering or leaving its enemy's ports

border states during the Civil War, a state that allowed slavery but remained in the Union: Delaware, Kentucky, Maryland, and Missouri

erode to eat into or wear away

Name _____ Class _____ Date _____

TOPIC 7 LESSON 4
Lesson Summary
AFRICAN AMERICANS AND THE WAR

MODIFIED CORNELL NOTES

With the slavery debate ongoing, Union officers had to decide what to do with enslaved African Americans who came under their control. One general declared them to be **contraband**, or captured war supplies. Another declared the slaves free, but Lincoln reversed that order, fearing retaliation from the border states. Lincoln secretly began working on a plan for the **emancipation** of enslaved African Americans living in Confederate states.

Confederate General Lee attempted to lead a pro-Confederate uprising in Maryland. On September 8, Lee issued the "Proclamation to the People of Maryland," which invited them to ally themselves with the South. Marylanders responded to the invitation with little enthusiasm, and Lee's proclamation failed.

Union and Confederate troops met at Sharpsburg, Maryland, on September 17 to fight the Battle of Antietam. It became the bloodiest day of the war with more than 23,000 soldiers dead or wounded.

On September 22, 1862, following the Battle of Antietam, Lincoln formally issued the Emancipation Proclamation. It stated that, as of January 1, 1863, all slaves in states in rebellion against the United States would be forever free. His decree did not apply to loyal border states. Although the Emancipation Proclamation did not actually free a single slave, it was an important turning point in the war. For northerners, it redefined the war as being "about slavery." For southerners, the call to free the slaves prevented any chance for a negotiated end to the war.

At the start of the war, many African Americans in the North were eager to fight but had been turned down. In the summer of 1862, Congress passed the Militia Act, mandating that black soldiers be accepted into the military. After the Emancipation Proclamation, the Union began to actively recruit black troops. The governor of Massachusetts supported the formation of the all-black 54th Massachusetts Regiment. Although African American troops distinguished themselves on the battlefield, they still faced **prejudice**. If captured, they would be killed. Enslaved African Americans in the South also played an important role in the war, often finding ways to help Union forces.

Lesson Vocabulary

contraband supplies captured from an enemy during wartime

emancipation the act or process of freeing someone from someone else's control

prejudice unfair feeling of dislike or hatred of a person or group of people based on characteristics such as race, religion, gender, or ethnicity

Name _____ Class _____ Date _____

Topic 7 Lesson 5
Lesson Summary
EVERYDAY LIFE DURING THE WAR

MODIFIED CORNELL NOTES

The war had a huge impact on northern industry. As demand for clothing, arms, and other supplies spiked, industry became more mechanized. To raise funds for the war, the government introduced an **income tax** of 3 percent on all income over $800 a year. This tax increased as the war continued. The Union also raised **tariffs**. The biggest source of wartime funds came from the sale of **bonds**. To increase the amount of cash in circulation, Congress passed the Legal Tender Act in 1862, creating the nation's first single, common currency.

Also in 1862, Congress passed the Homestead Act, making western land available at very low cost to those who would farm it. In 1863, the Union instituted **conscription**, or the draft. Under this system, any white man between the ages of 20 and 45 might be called for required military service. Many groups of northerners opposed the war effort. A **faction** calling themselves "Peace Democrats" criticized Lincoln's conduct and called for an end to the war. Their opponents dubbed them Copperheads, after a poisonous snake. Lincoln suspended the constitutional right of **habeas corpus**, which protects a person from being held in jail without being charged with a specific crime.

As the war dragged on, the South's economic and social underpinnings seemed in danger of collapse, due to the Union blockade of southern ports. Agriculture was often complicated by nearby military operations, and getting food to market was difficult because rivers and rail lines were often blocked. Like the Union, the Confederacy issued paper money, enacted conscription laws, seized private property, and suspended habeas corpus.

Many families suffered divided loyalties, with members fighting on different sides. New technology resulted in killing on a scale never before seen in America. Camp life was dangerous due to poor drinking water and lack of sanitation. Even worse were the prison camps. In both the North and the South, the most notable military role for women was nursing. In 1861, Clara Barton obtained permission to travel with army ambulances and assist in "distributing comforts to the sick and wounded" of both sides.

Lesson Vocabulary

income tax   a tax that must be paid by individuals and corporations based on money earned

tariff   a tax on imported goods

bond   a certificate bought from the government that promises to pay the holder back the purchase amount plus interest at a future date

conscription   the drafting of citizens into military service

faction   a group of people inside a political party or government working with a common cause against other such groups or against the main body

habeas corpus   a constitutional guarantee that no one can be held in prison without charges being filed

Copyright © by Pearson Education, Inc., or its affiliates. All Rights Reserved.

Name _____ Class _____ Date _____

**TOPIC 7
LESSON 6**

Lesson Summary
KEY CIVIL WAR BATTLES

MODIFIED CORNELL NOTES

The major focus of the Union's western campaign remained the Mississippi River. In the spring of 1863, Grant decided on a new approach in trying to capture Vicksburg, Mississippi. He cut Vicksburg off from its source of supply and then, after two failed attempts to storm the stronghold, he placed it under **siege**. Constant gunfire and lack of supplies weakened Vicksburg's defenders, and on July 4, 1863, the Confederate commander surrendered. This victory completed the Anaconda Plan of cutting the South in half.

The situation was different in the East, where Lincoln replaced General McClellan. McClellan's **successor**, General Ambrose Burnside, headed south, hoping to win a decisive victory over the Army of Northern Virginia. Lincoln quickly replaced Burnside with General Joseph Hooker, and in the spring, Hooker and Lee met at Chancellorsville, Virginia. Again the Confederates completely overwhelmed the Union army, but Lee lost Stonewall Jackson.

Lee sensed an opportunity to win international support, demoralize the Union, and perhaps even force an end to the war. He decided to invade the North, and in June 1863, his army crossed into Union territory in Pennsylvania. Under General George Meade, the Army of the Potomac set out to find the Confederates. On July 1, the two armies faced off in Gettysburg, Pennsylvania, in a battle that lasted for three days. On July 3, Confederate forces charged up Cemetery Ridge, only to be mowed down. The battle ended with over 50,000 dead and wounded. About half of these were Confederate—nearly a third of Lee's force. The South had suffered a devastating defeat. In November 1863, Lincoln came to the battlefield to dedicate a cemetery for the fallen soldiers. His Gettysburg Address described the United States as a single, unified nation.

In early 1864, Lincoln recalled Grant from the Mississippi Valley to take charge of the entire Union military effort. Grant used a strategy of **total war**. Part of that strategy was illustrated by the campaign of William Tecumseh Sherman. He cut a swath of destruction in his march across Georgia to the Atlantic. Sherman called the capture of Savannah his Christmas present for Lincoln.

Lesson Vocabulary

siege   a military tactic in which an enemy is surrounded and all supplies are cut off in an attempt to force a surrender

successor   a person or thing that follows another

total war   a military strategy in which an army attacks not only enemy troops but the economic and civilian resources that support them

Name _____ Class _____ Date _____

Topic 7 Lesson 7

Lesson Summary
IMPACT OF THE CIVIL WAR

MODIFIED CORNELL NOTES

If the Union captured Petersburg, Virginia, a vital railroad center, it would control all supply lines into the Confederate capital at Richmond. As at Vicksburg, Grant used siege tactics. He hoped to defeat Lee through **attrition**. Though Lee's forces struck effective blows against the Union troops, which suffered over 40,000 casualties, Lee had no replacements for the 28,000 men that Confederate forces lost. Southerners began to talk of peace.

In February, a party led by Confederate Vice President Alexander Stephens met with Lincoln to discuss a **feasible** end to the war, but these discussions produced no results. Congress had recently proposed the Thirteenth Amendment, which would outlaw slavery in the United States. The South was unwilling to accept a future without slavery. On April 2, Lee ordered a retreat from Petersburg. On April 9, 1865, Lee formally surrendered to Grant at Appomattox Court House, Virginia. On April 14, Lincoln was assassinated by John Wilkes Booth while attending a play at Ford's Theater. His death had a deep political impact, uniting his northern supporters and critics, who saw him as a hero and symbol of freedom.

When the Civil War began, it was unclear who would be victorious. However, the North was able to marshal its greater technological prowess, larger population, and more abundant resources. Meanwhile, the South used up its resources, unable to call upon fresh troops and supplies. In the long run, the North's Anaconda Plan succeeded. When opinion in the North was bitterly divided, Lincoln's steady leadership helped keep the nation together.

When the war was over, more than 600,000 Americans were dead. The Civil War ushered in the harsh reality of modern warfare, as ordinary citizens viewed the carnage of the battlefield through the photographs of Matthew Brady. The southern landscape was in shambles, with many people left homeless and in shock. African Americans were disoriented, but they also had a new sense of hope. In the North, the industrial boom that was fueled by the war continued. In the decades following the war, factories, banks, and cities underwent sweeping industrialization. Debates over states' rights did not end with the Civil War, although the war helped cement federal authority.

Lesson Vocabulary

attrition   the act of weakening and tiring out an enemy through constant attack

feasible   possible; practical

Name _____ Class _____ Date _____

Topic 7: Review Questions
SECTIONAL DIVISIONS AND THE CIVIL WAR

Answer the questions below using the information in the Lesson Summaries on the previous pages.

Lesson 1: Slavery Divides the Nation

1. Contrast the economies and ways of life that developed in the North and the South.
   _____
   _____

2. **Understand Effects** What effects did the Fugitive Slave Act have?
   _____
   _____

Lesson 2: Violence Escalates

3. What was the outcome of the Kansas-Nebraska Act?
   _____
   _____

4. **Compare and Contrast** Compare the positions of Abraham Lincoln and Stephen Douglas on the issue of slavery.
   _____
   _____

Lesson 3: The Civil War Begins

5. **Identify Causes and Effects** How did the split in the Democratic Party lead to Lincoln's victory in the 1860 election?
   _____
   _____

6. What events led to the outbreak of war?
   _____
   _____

Lesson 4: African Americans and the War

7. **Identify Effects** What effects did the Emancipation Proclamation have in the North and in the South?
   _____
   _____

8. How did African Americans contribute to the war effort?
   _____
   _____

Copyright © by Pearson Education, Inc., or its affiliates. All Rights Reserved.

Name _____ Class _____ Date _____

TOPIC 7 Review Questions
SECTIONAL DIVISIONS AND THE CIVIL WAR (continued)

Lesson 5: Everyday Life During the War

9. What effect did the Civil War have on northern industry?
   _____
   _____

10. **Identify Effects** What effect did the northern blockade have on the South?
    _____
    _____

Lesson 6: Key Civil War Battles

11. **Summarize** What events marked the major turning points in the Civil War? Explain.
    _____
    _____

12. Why was significant about the Gettysburg Address?
    _____
    _____

Lesson 7: Impact of the Civil War

13. **Recognize Sequence** What effect did the proposal of the Thirteenth Amendment have on discussions to end the war?
    _____
    _____

14. What factors enabled the North to win the Civil War?
    _____
    _____

Name _____ Class _____ Date _____

TOPIC 8
Note Taking Study Guide
RECONSTRUCTION

Focus Question: What were the goals of Reconstruction? What actions were taken or events occurred that advanced or slowed down those goals? What final outcomes resulted from these actions and events?

As you read, focus on the positive and negative changes that occurred during Reconstruction and the impact they had. Identify the new laws and programs that began during Reconstruction. Assess the impact of Reconstruction in achieving its goals.

Goals	Actions/Events	Outcome
Return southern states to Union	• •	Southern states rejoin the Union.
	• • • • •	
	• • • • • • •	

Copyright © by Pearson Education, Inc., or its affiliates. All Rights Reserved.

Name _____ Class _____ Date _____

TOPIC 8 LESSON 1

Lesson Summary
PLANS FOR RECONSTRUCTION CLASH

MODIFIED CORNELL NOTES

During the era of Reconstruction (1865–1877), the federal government struggled with how to return the southern states to the Union, rebuild the South's ruined economy, and promote the rights of former slaves. Some argued that states should be allowed to rejoin the Union quickly with few conditions. But many claimed that the defeated states should first satisfy certain **stipulations**, such as swearing loyalty to the federal government and adopting state constitutions that guaranteed freedmen's rights.

President Lincoln wanted to readmit southern states as soon as ten percent of a state's voters took a loyalty oath to the Union. "Radical Republicans" in Congress opposed this plan, insisting that the Confederates had committed crimes. Congress passed the Wade-Davis Bill in 1864. It required a majority of a state's prewar voters to swear loyalty before the state could be readmitted, and it demanded full equality for African Americans. Lincoln killed the bill with a "pocket veto." However, he supported the Freedmen's Bureau. Its goal was to provide food, clothing, healthcare, and education for both black and white refugees in the South.

Lincoln's assassination in April 1865 thrust his Vice President, Andrew Johnson, into the presidency. Johnson wanted to restore the political status of the southern states as quickly as possible. He did not want African Americans to have the vote and had little sympathy for their plight. All the southern states instituted **black codes**, laws that limited the rights of African Americans. When Congress sought to overturn them by passing the Civil Rights Act of 1866, Johnson vetoed it.

Violence against African Americans in the South increased. To protect freedmen's rights, Congress passed the Fourteenth Amendment, which guaranteed equality under the law for all citizens. The Military Reconstruction Act of 1867 divided the South into five military districts and set requirements for states to reenter the Union. A power struggle between Congress and the President continued. The House of Representatives voted to **impeach** Johnson in 1868. He escaped being removed from office by one vote. In 1869, the Fifteenth Amendment was passed. It forbids any state from denying suffrage on the grounds of race or color.

Lesson Vocabulary

stipulation the act of specifying a condition in an argument

black codes laws that restricted African Americans' rights and opportunities

impeach charge public official with misconduct

Lesson Summary
TOPIC 8 LESSON 2: RECONSTRUCTION CHANGES THE SOUTH

MODIFIED CORNELL NOTES

The era of Reconstruction brought many changes to the South. Millions of southern African American men were now voters, and many served as elected officials. They used their voting power to usher the Republican Party into the South. The Republican Party attracted people who sought change and challenge. **Scalawags** were white men who had been locked out of pre-Civil War politics by their wealthier neighbors. They found allies in **"carpetbaggers"**, or northern white or black men who relocated to the South.

Northern women, both white and black, had opportunities in the Reconstruction South that they could not pursue at home, including shaping the new public school system. Southerners opted for **segregation**, or separation of the races, in their school system. **Integration**—combining the schools—appealed to only the most radical white Republicans. Nevertheless, the beginning of a tax-supported public school system was a major Reconstruction success.

Many of the South's problems resulted from the uneven distribution of land. Wealth was defined by landownership. However, even owners of large tracts of land had no money with which to purchase supplies or pay workers. As a result, many southerners adopted one of three arrangements. Under the **sharecropping** system, a landowner dictated the crop and provided the sharecropper with a place to live and supplies in return for a "share" of the harvested crop. Under a **share-tenancy**, the farmworker chose what crop he would plant and bought his own supplies, then gave a share of the crop to the landowner. The most independent system was **tenant farming**, under which the tenant paid cash rent to the landowner and was free to choose his own crop and where to live.

(Continues on the next page.)

Lesson Vocabulary

scalawags negative term for a southern white person who supported the Republican Party after the Civil War

carpetbagger negative term for northerners who moved to the South after the Civil War

segregation forced separation, often by race

integration process of bringing people of different races, religions, and social classes together

sharecropping system in which a farmer tended a portion of a planter's land in return for a share of the crop

share-tenancy much like sharecropping, except that the farmer chose what crop he would plant and bought his own supplies

tenant farming system in which a farmer paid rent to a landowner for the use of the land

Lesson Summary
RECONSTRUCTION CHANGES THE SOUTH (continued)

TOPIC 8 LESSON 2

MODIFIED CORNELL NOTES

The more progress African Americans made, the more hostile white southerners became. Dozens of loosely organized groups of white southerners emerged to terrorize African Americans. The best known of these was the Ku Klux Klan. Racial violence grew even more widespread after the Fifteenth Amendment guaranteed all American men the right to vote. Congress took action, passing Enforcement Acts in 1870 and 1871. These acts made it a federal offense to interfere with a citizen's right to vote.

Topic 8, Lesson 3

Lesson Summary: Reconstruction's Impact

MODIFIED CORNELL NOTES

The continued cost of military operations in the South worried many people. Beginning in 1871, troops were withdrawn from the South. In 1872, the Freedmen's Bureau was dissolved. The death of a Radical Republican leader in 1874 symbolized an important **transition**. A generation of white reformers, forged by abolitionist fervor, had passed away. Without such leaders, northern racial prejudice reemerged. In a series of landmark cases, the Supreme Court chipped away at African American freedom in the 1870s. A group of southern Democrats put together a coalition to return the South to the rule of white men. The main focus of their strategy was compromise: finding common issues that would unite white southerners with the goal of regaining power in Congress. These compromisers have become known as Redeemers.

In the 1876 election, the Democratic candidate received 51 percent of the popular vote. When the Republicans demanded a recount, they found enough mistakes to swing the election. Rutherford B. Hayes won by one electoral vote in what became known as the Compromise of 1877. In return, the remaining federal troops were withdrawn from the South and southern states were guaranteed federal subsidies to build railroads and improve their ports. Reconstruction was over. Although it fell short of its goals, Reconstruction opened new opportunities for African Americans in the North and South. Constitutional amendments provided hope for full inclusion in American society, although it would take generations to use them to gain racial equality.

Black southerners now had the right to vote. New opportunities opened up for them. Perhaps the most important goal was education. Hundreds of schools and dozens of teachers' colleges enabled African Americans to learn to read. However, some white southerners focused their own frustrations on trying to reverse the gains African Americans had achieved during Reconstruction. Groups such as the Ku Klux Klan used terror and violence to intimidate African Americans. Many African American freedoms were whittled away. Congress passed the Civil Rights Act of 1875 to guarantee black patrons the right to ride trains and use public facilities. However, the Supreme Court ruled that the decision about who could use public accommodations was a local issue to be governed by state or local laws. Southern municipalities took advantage of this ruling to further limit the rights of African Americans.

(Continues on the next page.)

Lesson Vocabulary

transition the process of moving from one stage to another

Name _____ Class _____ Date _____

TOPIC 8 LESSON 3 — Lesson Summary
RECONSTRUCTION'S IMPACT (continued)

MODIFIED CORNELL NOTES

Even during the darkest days of Jim Crow, African Americans refused to accept their **status** as second-class citizens. They established black newspapers, women's clubs, fraternal organizations, schools and colleges, and political associations with the goal of securing their freedom. Former slave Ida B. Wells published the newspaper Free Speech. She wrote articles condemning the treatment of African Americans and criticizing lynching. Booker T. Washington argued that African Americans needed to accommodate themselves to segregation, build up economic resources, and establish reputations as hardworking and honest citizens. W.E.B. Du Bois criticized Washington and argued that African Americans should demand full and immediate equality.

Lesson Vocabulary

status   legal position or condition of a person, group, country, etc.

Name _____ Class _____ Date _____

TOPIC 8
Review Questions
RECONSTRUCTION

Answer the questions below using the information in the Lesson Summaries on the previous pages.

Lesson 1: Plans for Reconstruction Clash

1. What were the main goals of the Reconstruction of the South?
_____
_____

2. Identify Main Ideas What did Congress do to protect the rights of African Americans?
_____
_____

Lesson 2: Reconstruction Changes the South

3. How did Republicans gain control of elected government in the South during Reconstruction?
_____
_____

4. Identify Main Ideas How did African Americans' lives change during Reconstruction?
_____
_____

Lesson 3: Reconstruction's Impact

5. Identify Main Ideas Why did many people in the North stop supporting Reconstruction?
_____
_____

6. What were some of the successes of Reconstruction?
_____
_____

Name _____ Class _____ Date _____

TOPIC 9
Note Taking Study Guide
INDUSTRY AND IMMIGRATION

Focus Question: As the "new immigrants" moved to the United States what issues did they face as newcomers? How did they deal with those issues?

As you read, focus upon the new setting immigrants to the U.S. faced during the late 1800s. Identify the national problems that would pose challenges to immigrants as well as the issues they confronted because of their immigrant status. Record how immigrants, workers, and other Americans responded to those challenges.

The Challenges	The Responses

Name _____ Class _____ Date _____

TOPIC 9 LESSON 1
Lesson Summary
INNOVATION BOOSTS GROWTH

MODIFIED CORNELL NOTES

The Civil War encouraged industrial growth by challenging industries to make products more quickly and efficiently than before. The country's growth was also fueled by its vast supply of natural resources. In addition, industries had a huge workforce to fuel growth. After the Civil War, many Europeans and some Asians immigrated to the United States.

Entrepreneurs fueled industrialization. Capitalism is a system in which individuals own most businesses. The heroes of this system are **entrepreneurs**, or people who invest money in a product or enterprise in order to make a profit.

Government encouraged the success of businesses in the late 1800s. To encourage the buying of American goods, Congress enacted **protective tariffs**, or taxes that would make imported goods cost more than those made locally. The government also adopted **laissez-faire** policies, which allowed businesses to operate under minimal government regulation.

Thomas Edison received more than 1,000 **patents** for new inventions. Edison and his team invented the light bulb. George Westinghouse developed technology to send electricity over long distances. Electricity lit streets and powered homes and factories. Alexander Graham Bell patented the telephone. By 1900, there were more than one million telephones in the United States.

To meet the growing demand for goods, factory owners developed a system known as **mass production**, which allowed them to turn out large numbers of products quickly and inexpensively.

(Continues on the next page.)

Lesson Vocabulary

entrepreneurs   people who build and manage businesses or enterprises in order to make a profit, often risking their own money or livelihoods

protective tariff   taxes on imported goods making the price high enough to protect domestic goods from foreign competition

laissez-faire   a theory advocating minimal government interference in the economy

patent   official rights given by the government to an inventor for the exclusive right to develop, use, and sell an invention for a set period of time

mass production   production of goods in large numbers through the use of machinery and assembly lines

Copyright © by Pearson Education, Inc., or its affiliates. All Rights Reserved.

Name _____ Class _____ Date _____

TOPIC 9 LESSON 1

Lesson Summary
INNOVATION BOOSTS GROWTH (continued)

MODIFIED CORNELL NOTES

While industry boomed in some parts of the United States, the South grew more slowly and lagged behind the rest of the country. Before the Civil War, the South had shipped its raw materials abroad or to the North for processing. After the war, the South first had to repair the damages of war and then attempt to catch up with the North's industrial development. In the 1880s, northern money helped the South build its own factories. Southern leaders called for a "New South" and encouraged the expansion of southern rail lines.

However, the South could not keep pace with the North in industrial growth. The South had plenty of natural resources, but it did not have enough skilled labor and capital investment. Wages were low and most of the region's wealth remained in the hands of a few people.

Before the Civil War, most southern planters had concentrated on **cash crops**, such as cotton and tobacco, which they grew to sell. Cotton remained the centerpiece of southern agriculture. However, many European textile factories had found other suppliers during the war, so the price of cotton had fallen. In the 1890s, the boll weevil struck at cotton crops across the South, causing cotton to continue to be an issue in the South as the 1900s began.

Industrialization touched every aspect of American life. Farms became mechanized. Mass production meant people had easier access to goods. As the United States grew as an economic power, it became more involved in the affairs of other nations.

Lesson Vocabulary

cash crop   crop grown for sale

Name _____ Class _____ Date _____

Topic 9 Lesson 2
Lesson Summary
BIG BUSINESS RISES

MODIFIED CORNELL NOTES

To take advantage of larger markets, investors developed a form of group ownership known as a **corporation**. In a corporation, a number of people share ownership of a business. Corporations had access to huge amounts of money, allowing them to fund new technology or enter new industries.

Corporations worked to maximize profits in several ways. Some corporations tried to gain a **monopoly**, or complete control of a product or service. Other corporations worked to eliminate competition by forming **cartels**. In this arrangement, businesses making the same product agreed to limit their production and thus keep prices high. Another way to increase profits was to create a giant company with lower production costs. This system of consolidating many firms in the same business is called **horizontal integration**. John D. Rockefeller, Andrew Carnegie, and other businessmen also increased their power by gaining control of the many different business that make up all phases of a product's development. This process, called **vertical integration**, allowed businesses to reduce their costs and charge higher prices to competitors.

Consumers, workers, and the federal government gradually came to feel that systems like **trusts**, cartels, and monopolies gave powerful businesses an unfair advantage. At the same time, many people believed that business leaders served the nation positively. Factories, steel mills, and railroads provided jobs. The development of efficient business practices and industrialists' support for developing technology benefited the nation's economy and shaped the United States into a strong international leader. Finally, many business leaders were important philanthropists.

(Continues on the next page.)

Lesson Vocabulary

corporation company recognized as a legal unit that has rights and liabilities separate from each of its members

monopoly exclusive control by one company over an entire industry

cartel association of producers of a good or service that prices and controls stocks in order to monopolize the market

horizontal integration system of consolidating many firms in the same business

vertical integration system of consolidating firms involved in all steps of a product's manufacture

trust group of separate companies that are placed under the control of a single managing board in order to form a monopoly

Name _____ Class _____ Date _____

TOPIC 9 LESSON 2
Lesson Summary
BIG BUSINESS RISES (continued)

MODIFIED CORNELL NOTES

Charles Darwin's theory of survival of the fittest was applied to the world of American capitalism and was called Social Darwinism. People used Social Darwinism to justify all sorts of beliefs and conditions, such as discrimination.

The federal government slowly became involved in regulating trusts. In 1890, the Senate passed the Sherman Antitrust Act. This act outlawed any trust that operated in restraint of trade or commerce among several states.

Copyright © by Pearson Education, Inc., or its affiliates. All Rights Reserved.

Lesson Summary
THE ORGANIZED LABOR MOVEMENT

Topic 9, Lesson 3

Industrial growth produced wealth for business owners. However, some factory workers toiled long hours in dirty workhouses known as **sweatshops**. Many miners were forced to live in communities near their workplace. The housing in these **company towns** was owned by the business and rented to employees. By the time workers received wages, they owed most of their income to the company. As early as the 1820s, factory workers tried to gain more power against employers by using the technique of collective bargaining. One form of **collective bargaining** was the strike.

In the 1830s, a movement called socialism spread throughout Europe. Socialism is an economic and political philosophy that favors public, instead of private, control of property and income. Many labor activists borrowed ideas from socialism to support their goals.

The Knights of Labor, a labor union founded in 1869, included all workers of any trade, skilled or unskilled. The union sought broad social reform. In 1881, Terence V. Powderly became its leader.

In 1886, Samuel Gompers formed the American Federation of Labor (AFL). Unlike the Knights of Labor, the AFL focused on specific workers' issues, such as wages, working hours, and conditions.

On May 1, 1886, thousands of workers mounted a national demonstration for an eight-hour workday. Strikes erupted in several cities. At Haymarket Square in Chicago, frenzy broke out when a protester threw a bomb, killing a policeman. Dozens more people were killed. As a result of the Haymarket Riot, employers and many Americans associated union activities with violence.

(Continues on the next page.)

Lesson Vocabulary

sweatshop   small factories where employees have to work long hours under poor conditions for little pay

company town   communities in which residents rely upon one company for jobs, housing, and buying goods

collective bargaining   process in which employers negotiate with labor unions about hours, wages, and other working conditions

Topic 9 Lesson 3

Lesson Summary
THE ORGANIZED LABOR MOVEMENT (continued)

MODIFIED CORNELL NOTES

The Homestead Strike was part of a wave of steelworkers' and miners' strikes that took place as economic depression crept across America. In each case, federal troops were called in.

In 1893, Eugene V. Debs, leader of the American Railway Union, called for a nationwide strike against the Pullman Company. By June 1894, nearly 300,000 railworkers had walked off their jobs. The Pullman Strike escalated, halting both railroad traffic and mail delivery. Federal troops were sent in to end the strike. Afterward, an important trend developed. The federal government regularly supported businesses over labor unions.

Name _____ Class _____ Date _____

TOPIC 9
LESSON 4

Lesson Summary
THE NEW IMMIGRANTS

MODIFIED CORNELL NOTES

Many early American immigrants were Protestants from northern and western Europe or German and Irish Catholics. Many were skilled, educated, and came as families to work on farms. In the 1870s, "new" immigrants from southern and eastern Europe came to America. They often came alone, were unskilled and poor, Catholic or Jewish, and settled in cities rather than on farms.

Two types of factors lead to immigration. Push factors compel people to leave their homes. These include famine, war, and persecution. Pull factors, such as economic opportunities or religious freedom, draw people to a new place. Land reform and low prices for grain pushed farmers in Mexico, Poland, China, and Italy to leave. Wars in China and eastern Europe, and religious persecution in eastern Europe were also push factors. Inexpensive land and employment opportunities were examples of pull factors.

Most immigrants traveled in **steerage**, the crowded and dirty lower decks of steamships. There, illness spread quickly. Ship owners did a preliminary medical screening before passengers boarded, but immigration officials still met ships at American ports to determine who could stay. Immigrants had to be healthy and prove that they had money, a skill, or a sponsor. Beginning in 1892, most European immigrants were processed at Ellis Island in New York Harbor. Chinese and other Asian immigrants were processed at Angel Island, which opened in 1910 in San Francisco Bay.

Volunteer organizations tried to help immigrants blend into the **"melting pot"** of American society. Still, many immigrants held on to their traditions. Newcomers often faced **nativism**, the belief that native-born white Americans were superior to newcomers. Immigrants competed for jobs and housing, and their religious and cultural differences made native-born Americans suspicious. Hostility toward Chinese laborers led Congress to pass the Chinese Exclusion Act in 1882, limiting the civil rights of Chinese immigrants and forbidding their naturalization. Despite opposition, immigrants fueled industrial growth, elected politicians, and made their traditions part of American culture.

Lesson Vocabulary

steerage   third-class accommodations on a steamship

"melting pot"   society in which people of different nationalities assimilate to form one culture

nativism   inclination to favor native inhabitants as opposed to immigrants

Name _____ Class _____ Date _____

MODIFIED CORNELL NOTES

TOPIC 9 LESSON 5
Lesson Summary
A NATION OF CITIES

America went through **urbanization** in the late nineteenth century. The number of cities and their populations greatly increased. Major cities were clustered in the Northeast, on the Pacific Coast, and along Midwestern waterways. These centers of manufacturing and transportation were connected by new railroad lines.

In addition to immigrants looking for factory work, many rural-to-urban migrants moved to cities. Making a living by farming was increasingly difficult, and cities offered excitement and variety. Cities also offered great job possibilities for women. Children had the opportunity to attend school.

To meet increased demands for water, sewers, schools, and safety in growing cities, Americans developed new technologies. These innovations included electric trolleys, subways, and **skyscrapers**, tall buildings that housed large numbers of offices. Elisha Otis developed a safe elevator that would not fall if the lifting rope broke. Streetcars powered by electricity revolutionized transportation. **Mass transit**, public transportation systems capable of carrying a large number of people inexpensively, reshaped the nation. Those who could afford it moved to cleaner and quieter streetcar **suburbs** on the outskirts of cities and rode mass transit into the city for work and entertainment.

City planners created different zones for heavy industry, financial institutions, and residences. They also built public places, such as libraries, government buildings, universities, and parks. Landscape engineer Frederick Law Olmsted was hired to design a number of parks, including New York City's Central Park.

With the growth of cities came a number of problems. Cities were filthy and filled with trash. Most urban workers lived in overcrowded, low-cost multifamily housing called **tenements**. With few windows and little sanitation, they were unhealthy and dangerous places. Open fireplaces and gas lighting caused fires to quickly rip through cities. Unlit streets also posed dangers to those coming from or going to work. In response, many cities created firefighting teams and police forces. City planners began regulating housing, sanitation, and sewers.

Lesson Vocabulary

urbanization   expansion of cities and/or an increase in the number of people living in them

skyscrapers   very tall buildings

mass transit   public transportation systems that carry large numbers of people

suburbs   residential areas surrounding a city

tenements   multistory buildings divided into apartments to house as many residents as possible

Name _____ Class _____ Date _____

TOPIC 9 LESSON 6
Lesson Summary
NEW WAYS OF LIFE

MODIFIED CORNELL NOTES

In *The Gilded Age*, novelist Mark Twain depicted American society in the late 1800s as gilded, or having a rotten core but being covered with gold paint. Most Americans were not as cynical. More people worked for wages, and more products were available at lower prices, leading to a culture of **conspicuous consumerism**.

Department stores opened in the late 1850s. They used advertising to sell high-quality goods at fair prices. The postal service lowered shipping rates and offered free rural delivery, leading to a mail-order boom. Companies began creating trademarks with distinctive logos, and consumers began buying brand-name goods for the first time.

Transportation, advertising, and communication helped create a **mass culture** in which Americans became more and more alike in their consumption patterns. Household gadgets, toys, and food preferences were often the same from house to house. Newspapers both reflected and helped create mass culture, including Joseph Pulitzer's morning paper, the *World*. Pulitzer believed that newspapers should inform people and stir up controversy. William Randolph Hearst mimicked Pulitzer's sensationalist tactics in his newspaper, the *Morning Journal*. However, some novelists like Horatio Alger focused on moral issues. Ethnic and special-interest publications catered to urban dwellers, especially immigrants. Newspapers were successful, in part, because more people could read. Public education expanded rapidly, and by 1900, the literacy rate reached nearly 90 percent.

Urban areas became centers for new types of entertainment. Amusement parks were built close to cities around the country. Touring outdoor shows like "Buffalo Bill's Wild West Show" drew crowds. Religious-inspired entertainment, including the Chautauqua Circuit, also grew in popularity. **Vaudeville** shows, made up of musical drama, songs, and off-color comedy, were seen throughout the country. Movie theaters introduced motion pictures, charging a nickel for admission. Baseball, horse racing, bicycle racing, boxing, and football became popular spectator sports.

Lesson Vocabulary

conspicuous consumerism purchasing of goods and services with the purpose of impressing others

mass culture similar cultural patterns throughout a society as a result of the spread of transportation, communication, and advertising

vaudeville type of show that included dancing, singing, and comedy sketches and became popular in the late nineteenth century

Copyright © by Pearson Education, Inc., or its affiliates. All Rights Reserved.

Name _____ Class _____ Date _____

TOPIC 9: Review Questions
INDUSTRY AND IMMIGRATION

Answer the questions below using the information in the Lesson Summaries on the previous pages.

Lesson 1: Innovation Boosts Growth

1. What was the benefit of mass production?
   _____
   _____

2. **Identify Causes** How did entrepreneurs encourage industrialization?
   _____
   _____

Lesson 2: Big Business Rises

3. List two reasons some people had favorable opinions about the impact of big business.
   _____
   _____

4. **Identify Supporting Details** Name two methods that businesses used to increase their profits.
   _____
   _____

Lesson 3: The Organized Labor Movement

5. How did company towns negatively impact the workers who lived in them?
   _____
   _____

6. **Compare and Contrast** How did the goals of the Knights of Labor differ from those of the AFL?
   _____
   _____

Lesson 4: The New Immigrants

7. Describe the pull factors that drew immigrants to America.
   _____
   _____

8. **Identify Main Ideas** Discuss the challenges immigrants faced in America.
   _____
   _____

Name _____ Class _____ Date _____

TOPIC 9 — Review Questions
INDUSTRY AND IMMIGRATION (continued)

Lesson 5: A Nation of Cities

9. Why did people move to cities?
_____
_____

10. **Identify Main Ideas** Describe the problems caused by rapid growth and the steps that cities took to solve them.
_____
_____

Lesson 6: New Ways of Life

11. Describe how a mass culture developed in America.
_____
_____

12. **Identify Main Ideas** What forms of entertainment were popular in the late 1800s?
_____
_____

Name _____ Class _____ Date _____

TOPIC 10
Note Taking Study Guide
CHALLENGES IN THE LATE 1800s

Focus Question: What challenges did different ethnic groups face in the West?

The United States has always included many groups from many parts of the world. Sometimes there has been conflict between groups. As white settlers moved into the West, tensions flared with other groups. Fill in the graphic organizer to show at least two examples of the challenges faced by Native Americans, Mexican Americans, and Chinese Americans.

- Native Americans
- Mexican Americans
- **Challenging Discrimination**
- Chinese immigrants

Name _____ Class _____ Date _____

Topic 10 Lesson 1
Lesson Summary
AMERICAN INDIANS UNDER PRESSURE

MODIFIED CORNELL NOTES

By the end of the Civil War, about 25,000 American Indians lived in the region west of the Mississippi River known as "The Great American Desert." Geography influenced cultural diversity, but all American Indian cultures saw themselves as part of nature and considered it sacred. By contrast, many whites viewed the land as a resource to produce wealth. In the early 1800s, the government began to move Native Americans out of the way of white settlers. Things changed when gold and silver were discovered in Indian Territory. In 1851, the government began to restrict American Indians to smaller areas. By the late 1860s, they were forced to live on **reservations**, where they lacked adequate resources.

In 1864, Colorado militia attacked an unarmed camp of Cheyenne and Arapaho. The Sand Creek Massacre, as it came to be known, spawned more warfare between Plains Indians and white settlers. When gold was discovered in the Black Hills, the Sioux, led by Chiefs Crazy Horse and Sitting Bull, tried to drive white prospectors out of Sioux lands. At the Battle of Little Big Horn in June 1876, the Sioux killed all the United States Army cavalry forces led by George Custer. In 1877, the Nez Percés tried to escape to Canada when the federal government wanted to relocate them to a smaller reservation. The Nez Percés were captured just short of the border and relocated to a barren reservation in Oklahoma. Their leader, Chief Joseph, traveled twice to Washington, D.C., to lobby for mercy for his people. In 1890, hostilities broke out at Wounded Knee, South Dakota, over a religious revival based on the Ghost Dance. The cavalry outgunned the Indians.

Policymakers hoped that American Indians would become farmers and **assimilate** into national life by adopting the culture and civilization of whites. In 1887, Congress passed the Dawes General Allotment Act. It replaced the reservation system with a system under which each American Indian family was granted a 160-acre farmstead. To help speed assimilation, missionaries and other reformers established boarding schools where Indian children were taught to live by the rules of white Americans.

Lesson Vocabulary

reservations public lands where Native Americans were required to live by the federal government

assimilate absorb into the main culture of a society

Name _____ Class _____ Date _____

TOPIC 10 LESSON 2
Lesson Summary
THE WEST IS TRANSFORMED

MODIFIED CORNELL NOTES

Mining was the first great boom in the West. Mining camps sprang up quickly.

As industry in the West grew, the need for a **transcontinental railroad** linking the East and the West became apparent. Congress supported its construction in two ways: It provided money in the form of loans and made **land grants**, which gave builders wide stretches of land, alternating on each side of the track route. Work on the railroad began in 1863 and was completed in 1869. Railroads had far-reaching effects. They tied the nation together, moved products and people across the continent, and spurred industrial development. They also stimulated the growth of towns and cities and intensified the demand for American Indian land.

Cattle ranching was another western boom. With railroads capable of moving meat to eastern markets, the race was on for land and water. At first, cattle were raised on the **open-range** system. Property was not separated by fences, and cattle were branded for identification. Cowboys learned much from the Mexican vaqueros. By the mid-1880s, the heyday of open-range ranching came to an end.

The Great Plains was the last part of the country to be heavily settled by whites. Under the Homestead Act of 1862, the government offered farm plots to homesteaders. Some new settlers were formers slaves called "Exodusters." They followed an exodus out of bondage to a new "promised land" in Kansas and Oklahoma, where they planted crops and founded several all-black towns.

Chinese immigrants faced racial prejudice. Congress passed the Chinese Exclusion Act, prohibiting Chinese laborers from entering the country. Chinese "immigrants" turned to the federal courts. In 1898, the Supreme Court ruled that individuals of Chinese descent who were born in America could not be stripped of their citizenship.

Mexican Americans also struggled against discrimination. Despite guaranteed property rights, many Mexicans lost their lands after the Mexican-American War because they were unable to prove ownership. In the late 1880s and early 1890s, Las Gorras Blancas (the White Caps) fought back by engaging in guerilla warfare against the railroads and large ranchers.

Lesson Vocabulary

transcontinental railroad   rail link between the eastern and the western United States

land grants   land designated by the federal government for building schools, roads, or railroads

open-range   method of ranching in which the rancher allowed his or her livestock to roam and graze over a vast area of grassland

Name _____ Class _____ Date _____

TOPIC 10 LESSON 3

Lesson Summary
CORRUPTION PLAGUES THE NATION

MODIFIED CORNELL NOTES

Inaction and political corruption characterized politics during the Gilded Age. Neither Democrats nor Republicans controlled the White House and both houses of Congress for more than two years in a row, making it difficult to pass new laws. Presidents during this era seemed weak and lacked integrity.

Political parties reached into nearly every ward and precinct in every city. Under the **spoils system**, politicians gave government jobs to loyal party workers without consideration of their qualifications. Government officials could and did use federal contracts to convince people to vote for their candidates.

A number of prominent figures promoted reforming the civil service system, a system that would include federal jobs in the executive branch. Under a reformed civil service, government workers would be offered jobs based on their expertise and keep those jobs regardless of which political party won the election. After President James Garfield was assassinated by a citizen who felt cheated out of a job, Vice President Chester Arthur signed the Pendleton Civil Service Act in 1883. This act established a **civil service** commission. The commission wrote an exam that all who sought government employment had to take before being hired. Getting a job was based on how well one did on the exam, not on one's political affiliation and connections.

Two economic issues created a political divide during the Gilded Age: the tariff and the monetary policy. Republicans favored a high tariff, arguing that it would promote job growth and allow American industry to grow. Democrats believed that high tariffs would raise prices and make it harder for American farmers to sell their goods abroad.

Disagreement flared over the gold standard, the use of gold as the basis of the nation's currency. Bankers and those in international trade feared the use of silver for money would undermine the economy. Farmers argued that the rejection of silver money would lead to declining prices and financial ruin. Congress passed the Coinage Act of 1873, which ended the minting of silver coins, but after protest, it authorized minting of silver dollars.

Lesson Vocabulary

political parties   a political party's organization that wins voter loyalty and guarantees power to a small group of leaders, who often abuse it for their own gain

spoils system   practice of the political party in power giving jobs and appointments to its supporters, rather than to people based on their qualifications

civil service   government departments and their non-elected employees

Name _____ Class _____ Date _____

MODIFIED CORNELL NOTES

TOPIC 10 LESSON 4
Lesson Summary
FARM ISSUES AND POPULISM

In the 1870s, Texas farmers began to organize and to **negotiate** as a group for lower prices for supplies. Local organizations joined to form the Farmers' Alliance. Alliance members tried to force railroads to lower freight prices. They also wanted the government to regulate the interest that banks could charge for loans.

Between 1870 and 1895, farm prices fell sharply. At the same time, the cost of doing business increased. Many farmers **mortgaged** their farms to survive. Farmers blamed big business, especially the railroads and banks, for their problems. They believed that railroads charged whatever rates they wanted and that banks set interest rates too high.

In 1867, Oliver H. Kelley, a Minnesota farmer and businessman, organized the Grange, an organization of farmers that grew to nearly a million members. It was one of a network of organizations created to solve farmers' problems. The Grange provided education and called for the regulation of railroad and **grain elevator** rates. Grangers also prompted the federal government to establish the Interstate Commerce Commission (ICC) to oversee interstate transportation.

Farmers' Alliances took up the call for reform in the late 1870s. They formed cooperatives to collectively sell crops and called on the federal government to establish "sub-treasuries," or postal banks, to provide farmers with low-interest loans.

The spread of the Farmers' Alliances culminated with the creation of the Populist Party, or People's Party, in 1892. The party grew rapidly, putting pressure on the two major political parties to consider their demands. They called for the coinage of silver, or **"free silver,"** to fight low prices. To combat high costs, they demanded government ownership of railroads. In the 1892 election, the Populists elected several governors and senators, and 10 members of Congress. Their presidential candidate received more than one million votes.

Following this success, Populists were forced to decide whether to nominate their own presidential candidate or to endorse Democratic Party nominee William Jennings Bryan for the 1896 election. They chose to endorse Bryan, who supported many Populist proposals.

Bryan lost the election to Republican candidate William McKinley, partly because his emphasis on monetary reform, especially free silver, did not appeal to urban workers. The Populist decision to endorse Bryan weakened the party at the local and state levels. The party never recovered, and by the early 1900s, it had disappeared as a viable alternative to the two major political parties.

Lesson Vocabulary

negotiate to arrange or bring about a settlement of a matter

mortgage to borrow money against a piece of property by a legal agreement against a piece of property

grain elevator a building for storing grain

free silver a monetary policy that linked the supply of U.S. dollars to silver rather than gold

Name _____ Class _____ Date _____

TOPIC 10: Review Questions
CHALLENGES IN THE LATE 1800s

Answer the questions below using the information in the Lesson Summaries on the previous pages.

Lesson 1: American Indians Under Pressure

1. Who was Chief Joseph?

2. **Recognize Sequence** How did life change for Native Americans after gold and silver were discovered in Indian Territory?

Lesson 2: The West Is Transformed

3. Who were the Exodusters?

4. **Identify Main Ideas** Why were early settlers attracted to the West?

Lesson 3: Corruption Plagues the Nation

5. What is the term for the use of gold as a nation's currency?

6. **Identify Main Ideas** Discuss two economic issues that were important to politics during the Gilded Age.

Lesson 4: Farm Issues and Populism

7. What candidate did Populists endorse in the 1896 presidential election?

8. **Identify Causes and Effects** Describe the problems that led farmers to create groups such as the Grange.

Name _____ Class _____ Date _____

TOPIC 11 — Note Taking Study Guide
AMERICA COMES OF AGE

Focus Question: What specific areas of American life did Progressives believe needed to be reformed and how did they want to solve those problems?

As you read, focus upon the problems that Progressives recognized and their solutions to those problems.

Problem	Solution

Name _____ Class _____ Date _____

TOPIC 11, LESSON 1

Lesson Summary
PROGRESSIVES DRIVE REFORM

MODIFIED CORNELL NOTES

Industrialization, urbanization, and immigration brought many benefits to America, but they also produced challenging social problems. Progressivism was a social movement that arose in the 1890s to tackle these problems. Journalists whose stories dramatized the need for reform were called **muckrakers**. One leading muckraker was Lincoln Steffens, a magazine editor who published stories about political corruption. Another was Jacob Riis, a photographer whose pictures revealed life in urban slums. Novelist Frank Norris showed how the Southern Pacific Railroad kept a stranglehold on California farmers in *The Octopus*. Upton Sinclair's novel *The Jungle* revealed the unsafe and unsanitary conditions of Chicago meatpacking plants.

The work of the muckrakers increased popular support for progressivism and helped the Progressives bring about reforms. Laws were passed to end child labor and break up monopolies and trusts. After a fire at a garment factory killed nearly 150 workers, Progressives were able to get laws passed to protect worker safety.

Many reformers thought that Christianity should be the basis of social reform. These followers of the Social Gospel believed that society would improve if people followed the Bible's teachings about charity and justice. One form of charity was the **settlement house**, which offered services for the poor such as child care and classes in English. Hull House in Chicago was a famous settlement house founded by Jane Addams. Her work inspired others to help solve the problems of the urban poor by becoming social workers.

(Continues on the next page.)

Lesson Vocabulary

muckraker   writer who uncovers and exposes misconduct in government or business

settlement house   community center organized at the turn of the twentieth century to provide social services to the urban poor

Name _____ Class _____ Date _____

MODIFIED CORNELL NOTES

TOPIC 11 LESSON 1
Lesson Summary
PROGRESSIVES DRIVE REFORM (continued)

In order to reform politics and remove corrupt governments, Progressives pushed for a number of new laws. Dynamic leaders such as Wisconsin Governor Robert La Follette created tools to limit the power of political bosses and business interests. Reformers created the **direct primary** so citizens, not political bosses, could select nominees for upcoming elections. The **initiative** gave people the power to put a proposed new law directly on the ballot. The **referendum** allowed citizens to approve or reject laws passed by a legislature. The **recall** gave voters the power to remove elected officials from office before their terms ended. These reforms brought about by Progressives continue to affect society today.

Lesson Vocabulary

direct primary election in which citizens themselves vote to select nominees for upcoming elections

initiative process in which citizens put a proposed new law directly on the ballot

referendum process that allows citizens to approve or reject a law passed by a legislature

recall process by which voters can remove elected officials from office before their term ends

Copyright © by pearson Education, Inc., or its affiliates. All Rights Reserved.

Name _____ Class _____ Date _____

TOPIC 11 LESSON 2
Lesson Summary
WOMEN GAIN RIGHTS

MODIFIED CORNELL NOTES

In the early 1900s, a growing number of women sought to do more than fulfill their roles as wives and mothers. Many went to college to prepare for careers in teaching and nursing. Women had already won a shorter workday, but reformers saw the need for more changes. Florence Kelley believed that unfair prices for household goods hurt women and their families, so she helped found the National Consumers League (NCL). The NCL labeled products made in safe workplaces. The NCL also asked the government to improve food and workplace safety and assist the underemployed.

Women continued to fight for the right to vote, to own property, and to receive an education. Although women failed to gain the vote, the number of women attending college jumped dramatically.

Women also sought changes in the home. With the **temperance movement**, led by the Women's Christian Temperance Union (WCTU), women tried to reduce or end the consumption of alcohol. Members of the WCTU blamed alcohol for some men's abuse and neglect of their families. Margaret Sanger sought a different change. She thought that family life and women's health would improve if mothers had fewer children. Sanger opened the nation's first birth-control clinic. Ida B. Wells established the National Association of Colored Women, which helped African American families by providing childcare and education.

One of progressivism's boldest goals was women's **suffrage**, or the right to vote. This fight was started in the 1860s but was re-energized by Carrie Chapman Catt in the 1890s. Catt toured the country encouraging women to join the National American Woman Suffrage Association (NAWSA). This group lobbied Congress for the right to vote and used the referendum process to try to get women the vote in several states. By 1918, this strategy had helped women get the vote in several states. Alice Paul was more vocal in her efforts. In 1917, she formed the National Women's Party (NWP), which staged protest marches and hunger strikes and even picketed the White House to demand the right to vote. When the United States entered World War I in 1917, the NAWSA supported the war effort. Its actions and those of the NWP convinced a growing number of legislators to support a women's suffrage amendment. This reform became official in 1920 as the Nineteenth Amendment. Women finally had the right to vote for President.

Lesson Vocabulary

temperance movement   movement aimed at stopping alcohol abuse and the problems created by it

suffrage   the right to vote

Name _____ Class _____ Date _____

Topic 11 Lesson 3
Lesson Summary
STRIVING FOR EQUALITY

MODIFIED CORNELL NOTES

The Progressive Era was not so progressive for nonwhite and immigrant Americans. Most Progressives were white Anglo-Saxon Protestant reformers who were indifferent or hostile to minorities.

Settlement houses and other civic groups played a big role in the **Americanization** efforts of many Progressives. Americanization occurred when Progressives encouraged everyone to follow white, middle-class ways of life.

Many Progressives shared the same prejudices against non-whites as other Americans. They agreed with so-called scientific theories that said that dark-skinned peoples had less intelligence than whites. They also supported segregation, or separation of the races, and laws to limit minority voting.

African American reformers responded in different ways to formal segregation and discrimination. For example, Booker T. Washington told blacks that the best way to win their rights was to be patient and to earn the respect of white Americans. W.E.B. Du Bois, on the other hand, said that blacks should demand immediately all the rights guaranteed by the Constitution.

W.E.B. Du Bois was a member of the Niagara Movement, a group that called for rapid progress and more education for blacks. After a race riot broke out in Illinois, its members joined with white reformers to form the National Association for the Advancement of Colored People (NAACP). The NAACP planned to use the court system to fight for the civil rights of African Americans, including the right to vote. The efforts of the NAACP mostly helped middle-class blacks, but the Urban League focused on poorer urban workers. It helped families buy clothes and books and helped factory workers and maids find jobs.

African Americans were not alone in seeking their rights. Individuals and organizations of diverse ethnic groups spoke out against injustice and created self-help agencies. Jews in New York City formed the Anti-Defamation League to defend themselves against verbal attacks and false statements. Mexican Americans in several states formed **mutualistas**, groups that gave loans and provided legal assistance to the poor.

Lesson Vocabulary

Americanization belief that assimilating immigrants into American society would make them more loyal citizens

mutualistas organized groups of Mexican Americans that make loans and provide legal assistance to other members of their community

Name _____ Class _____ Date _____

TOPIC 11 LESSON 4
Lesson Summary
REFORMERS IN THE WHITE HOUSE

MODIFIED CORNELL NOTES

Theodore Roosevelt was a war hero, seasoned politician, and a dedicated reformer when he became President in 1901. Roosevelt used the power of the federal government to take on big business, breaking up **trusts** he considered abusive. In 1906, Roosevelt convinced Congress to pass the Hepburn Act, which limited what railroads could charge for shipping.

Roosevelt put millions of acres of forests under federal control. Like the head of the Division of Forestry, Gifford Pinchot, Roosevelt believed in the "rational use" of forests. The forests would be protected as future sources of lumber. To help settle fights over sources of water in the West, Roosevelt pushed for passage of the National Reclamation Act. That law gave the government power to build and manage dams to control where and how water was used.

After two terms in office, Roosevelt wanted William Howard Taft to follow him. However, Taft did not follow the course Roosevelt had set, and Roosevelt became disappointed and, later, angry. He began to speak out against Taft, promoting what he called New Nationalism, a program to restore the government's trust-busting power. A group of Progressives created the Progressive Party and nominated Roosevelt as its candidate for President.

During the 1912 election, Roosevelt and Taft split the Republican Party vote, allowing Democrat Woodrow Wilson to win the election. Like Roosevelt, Wilson was a reformer who thought government should play an active role in the economy. He shaped his ideas into a three-part program he called the New Freedom.

First, Wilson tried to prevent manufacturers from charging unfairly high prices. He cut **tariffs** on imported goods, which made foreign goods more competitive in the United States and forced U.S. producers to charge fair prices.

Second, Wilson pushed Congress to pass the Federal Reserve Act. This law gave the government authority to supervise banks by placing national banks under the control of the Federal Reserve Board.

(Continues on the next page.)

Lesson Vocabulary

trust a combination of businesses formed to reduce competition

tariff a tax on imported or exported goods

Copyright © by Pearson Education, Inc., or its affiliates. All Rights Reserved.

Name _____ Class _____ Date _____

TOPIC 11 LESSON 4

Lesson Summary
REFORMERS IN THE WHITE HOUSE (continued)

MODIFIED CORNELL NOTES

Third, Wilson made sure that trusts did not behave unfairly. He persuaded Congress to create the Federal Trade Commission (FTC) to monitor business practices and stop false advertising and dishonest labeling.

Progressivism had a major impact on the nation. Political reforms expanded the power of voters. Economic reforms enabled the government to **regulate** corporations and banks in the interest of the public. **Consumer** protections gave the public confidence that the products they bought were not harmful. The government also began to manage natural resources all over the nation.

Lesson Vocabulary

regulate   to make rules or laws to govern or control
consumer   a person who buys and uses goods and services

Topic 11 Lesson 5

Lesson Summary
AMERICAN INFLUENCE GROWS

MODIFIED CORNELL NOTES

During the late 1800s, the United States began to acquire influence and territory outside of its continental borders. It pursued a policy of **imperialism**, or the use of economic, political, and military control over weaker territories. Many imperialist nations wanted colonies to serve as **extractive economies**. Raw materials would be removed from these colonies and sent to the home country. In America there was a surplus of goods. American industrialists would benefit because they could sell their commodities in new colonial markets around the world.

Alfred T. Mahan, a historian and officer in the United States Navy, called upon the government to build a large navy in order to protect American interests around the world. To justify imperialism, many imperialists used ideas of racial, national, and cultural superiority. One of these ideas was Social Darwinism, the belief that life is a competitive struggle and that some races are superior to others and more fit to rule. Historian Frederick J. Turner wrote that America needed a large amount of unsettled land to succeed. Some Americans felt that the nation should expand into foreign lands.

In 1853, Commodore Matthew Perry sailed a large naval force to Japan. Perry won the Japanese emperor's favor by showering him with lavish gifts. Within a year, Japan agreed to trade with the United States. In 1867, Secretary of State William Seward bought Alaska from Russia. The purchase almost doubled the size of the United States and provided timber, oil, and other natural resources. In Latin America, U.S. business owners sought to expand their trade and investments, which increased the U.S. sphere of influence.

The Hawaiian Islands had been economically linked to the United States for almost a century. American sugar planters owned much of Hawaiian land. They used their influence to exclude many Hawaiians from the voting process. Queen Liliuokalani, the ruler of Hawaii, tried to limit the political power of the white minority. In 1893, the planters overthrew the queen and set up a new government. The United States annexed Hawaii in 1898. The United States was abandoning isolationism and emerging as a new power on the global stage.

Lesson Vocabulary

imperialism   political, military, and economic domination of strong nations over weaker territories

extractive economies   economy in a colony where the colonizing country removed raw materials and shipped them back home to benefit its own economy

TOPIC 11 LESSON 6

Lesson Summary
THE SPANISH-AMERICAN WAR

MODIFIED CORNELL NOTES

At the end of the nineteenth century, tensions were rising between Spain and its colony in Cuba. Cuban patriot José Martí launched a war for independence from Spain in 1895. Many Americans supported the Cubans, whose struggle for freedom and democracy reminded Americans of their own struggle for independence.

Newspaper publishers Joseph Pulitzer and William Randolph Hearst heightened the public's dislike of the Spanish government. Their publications, known as the Yellow Press, pushed for war with Spain by printing exaggerated stories of Spanish atrocities. In February 1898, Hearst's *New York Journal* published a letter written by Spain's ambassador, which called McKinley a weak and stupid politician. The letter fueled American **jingoism**, or aggressive nationalism. Soon after, the American battleship *Maine* exploded in Havana harbor. The Yellow Press promptly accused Spain of blowing up the battleship. In April 1898, the U.S. Congress declared war on Spain, beginning the Spanish-American War.

In the Spanish-held Philippines, Commodore George Dewey quickly destroyed a large part of the Spanish fleet. While Dewey was defeating the Spanish navy, Filipino nationalists led by Emilio Aguinaldo were defeating the Spanish army. In August, Spanish troops surrendered to the United States.

Meanwhile, U.S. troops landed in Cuba in June 1898. Although the troops were poorly trained, wore unsuitable uniforms, and carried old, outdated weapons, they were successful. Spanish forces in Cuba surrendered to the United States. Future President Theodore Roosevelt organized a force known as the Rough Riders. Joined by African American soldiers from the Ninth and Tenth Cavalry regiments, the Rough Riders played a key role in the war.

In December 1898, Spain and the United States signed the Treaty of Paris, officially ending the Spanish-American War. Spain gave up control of Cuba, Puerto Rico, and the Pacific island of Guam. It also sold the Philippines to the United States.

During the Spanish-American War, Filipino nationalist Emilio Aguinaldo viewed America as an ally in the Filipino struggle for independence. However, when the United States kept possession of the Philippines after the war, Aguinaldo grew disillusioned. He helped organize an **insurrection**, or rebellion, against U.S. rule.

The Filipino insurgents relied on **guerrilla warfare** tactics, including surprise raids and hit-and-run attacks. In turn, the U.S. military used extraordinary measures to crush the rebellion. The war in the Philippines highlighted the rigors of fighting against guerilla insurgents. Nearly 5,000 Americans and 200,000 Filipinos were killed in the fighting.

Lesson Vocabulary

jingoism   aggressive nationalism; support for warlike foreign policy

insurrection   rebellion

guerrilla warfare   nontraditional combat methods

Name _____ Class _____ Date _____

TOPIC 11 LESSON 7 — Lesson Summary
THE UNITED STATES EMERGES AS A WORLD POWER

MODIFIED CORNELL NOTES

The United States also wanted to increase trade with China. By 1899, Britain, France, Germany, and Russia had carved China into distinct **spheres of influence**, or zones. Because the United States did not have a zone, this system of privileged access to Chinese markets threatened to limit American trade. U.S. Secretary of State John Hay made it clear that America demanded equal trade access.

In May 1900, a Chinese nationalist group launched the Boxer Rebellion in objection to the presence of foreigners. As the rebellion engulfed China, Secretary of State Hay reasserted America's Open Door Policy, which stated that the United States wanted free trade, not colonies, in China. A multinational force of European, American, and Japanese troops put down the uprising.

In 1905, President Roosevelt negotiated an end to the Russo-Japanese War. The President's intervention displayed America's growing role in world affairs.

Roosevelt promoted military preparedness to protect U.S. interests in Asia. In 1907, Roosevelt sent a force of navy ships, known as the Great White Fleet, on a cruise around the world to demonstrate America's increased military power.

After the Spanish-American War, the United States assumed control of Puerto Rico and Cuba. In 1900, the U.S. Congress passed the Foraker Act, which established a civil government in Puerto Rico. In 1917, Puerto Ricans gained more citizenship rights and greater control over their own legislature.

After assuming the presidency, Theodore Roosevelt promoted **"big stick" diplomacy**, which relied on a strong U.S. military to achieve America's goals. Roosevelt used this forceful approach to intimidate Colombia and gain control over the "Canal Zone" in Panama. America then built the Panama Canal, a waterway that connected the Atlantic and Pacific oceans.

In 1913, President Woodrow Wilson, who had criticized imperialism, promoted his policy of **"moral diplomacy."** Wilson promised that America would work to promote "human rights, national integrity, and opportunity."

Although he intended to take U.S. policy in a different direction, President Wilson nevertheless used the military on a number of occasions.

Lesson Vocabulary

spheres of influence   a region dominated and controlled by an outside power

"big stick" diplomacy   Theodore Roosevelt's policy of creating and using, when necessary, a strong military to achieve America's goals

"moral diplomacy"   Woodrow Wilson's statement that the U.S. would not use force to assert influence in the world, but would instead work to promote human rights

Copyright © by Pearson Education, Inc., or its affiliates. All Rights Reserved.

Name _____ Class _____ Date _____

TOPIC 11: Review Questions
AMERICA COMES OF AGE

Answer the questions below using the information in the Lesson Summaries on the previous pages.

Lesson 1: Progressives Drive Reform

1. How did settlement houses help the poor?
_____
_____

2. Identify Details List four muckrakers whose work in the 1890s helped increase the public's awareness about social and political problems, and describe their work.
_____
_____

Lesson 2: Women Gain Rights

3. What methods did reformers use to fight for women's suffrage?
_____
_____

4. Identify Main Ideas What goal did Margaret Sanger, Ida B. Wells, and Florence Kelley share?
_____
_____

Lesson 3: Striving for Equality

5. Why did Progressives not fight for the civil rights of minorities?
_____
_____

6. Main Idea and Details How did Booker T. Washington differ from W.E.B. Du Bois in his approach to civil rights?
_____
_____

Lesson 4: Reformers in the White House

7. Why did President Roosevelt and Gifford Pinchot want to protect forests?
_____
_____

8. Identify Main Ideas How were the Square Deal and the New Nationalism programs similar?
_____
_____

Topic 11 Review Questions
AMERICA COMES OF AGE (continued)

Lesson 5: American Influence Grows

9. How did Social Darwinism contribute to imperialism?

10. **Identify Causes** What led to the annexation of Hawaii?

Lesson 6: The Spanish-American War

11. What territories did Spain give up in the Treaty of Paris?

12. **Identify Causes and Effects** What was the effect of the Yellow Press on the American public?

Lesson 7: The United States Emerges as a World Power

13. What was the purpose of proclaiming the Open Door Policy?

14. **Recognize Sequence** Number the following events in chronological order: Great White Fleet sails; China carved into spheres of influence; Roosevelt negotiates "Gentlemen's Agreement"

Name _____ Class _____ Date _____

TOPIC 12
Note Taking Study Guide
WORLD WAR I AND THE 1920s

Focus Question: What toll did America's involvement in World War I take on various aspects of society?

As you read, note specific examples that support the idea that the Economy, Women, Soldiers, and Politics were all greatly impacted by American involvement in World War I.

- Effects of World War I
  - Economy
  - Role of Women
  - Toll on Soldiers
  - America's Place in the World

Name _____ Class _____ Date _____

TOPIC 12 LESSON 1
Lesson Summary
AMERICA ENTERS WORLD WAR I

MODIFIED CORNELL NOTES

Although there had been no major wars, the 50 years before World War I were not tranquil. Nationalism renewed old grudges among countries. **Militarism**, or glorification of the military, eventually produced an arms race between Germany and Britain at sea and among Germany, France, and Russia on land.

In addition to strengthening their military power, European leaders prepared for war by forming alliances. Germany, Austria-Hungary, and Italy formed the Triple Alliance. Opposing them were France, Russia, and Great Britain, which formed the Triple Entente. In 1914, a Serbian youth assassinated Francis Ferdinand, the archduke of Austria-Hungary. War spread as European countries entered the fighting to help their allies. Russia came to the aid of Serbia against Austria. Germany declared war on Russia. France, Russia's ally, declared war on Germany. After Germany declared war on Belgium, Great Britain declared war on Germany. World War I had begun.

Although fighting went on in Eastern Europe, the Middle East, and other parts of the world, the Western Front in France became the critical battle front. German soldiers settled onto high ground, dug trenches, and fortified their position. The French and British then dug their own trenches. A stalemate developed and the war dragged on for years. New military technology, including machine guns and poison gas, led to millions of **casualties**.

As the war continued in Europe, President Woodrow Wilson called for Americans to remain impartial. However, Germany's brutal invasion of Belgium swayed American opinion against Germany. Americans also protested when a German submarine, or **U-boat**, sank the British passenger liner Lusitania.

In January 1917, German Foreign Minister Arthur Zimmermann sent a telegram to Mexico proposing an alliance between Germany and Mexico. The Zimmermann note was intercepted by the British, who gave it to American authorities. When the telegram was published, Americans were shocked by its contents. Next, Germany announced unrestricted submarine warfare against Britain. On April 6, 1917, the U.S. Congress declared war on Germany.

Lesson Vocabulary

militarism glorification of the military.

casualties soldiers killed, wounded, or missing

U-boat German submarine

Name _____ Class _____ Date _____

TOPIC 12 LESSON 2
Lesson Summary
THE HOME FRONT DURING WORLD WAR I

MODIFIED CORNELL NOTES

When the United States entered World War I, its army was only a fraction of the size of European armies. To build the army, Congress passed the Selective Service Act, which authorized a draft of young men for military service in Europe.

While the Selective Service Commission raised an army, the War Industries Board (WIB), headed by Bernard Baruch, regulated all industries engaged in the war effort. The WIB also urged Americans to conserve food as a patriotic gesture. As head of the Food Administration, future President Herbert Hoover set high prices for food to encourage farmers to increase production.

In 1917, many Americans questioned U.S. involvement in the war. The Committee on Public Information (CPI) worked to convince the American public that the war effort was a just cause. George Creel, the director of the CPI, combined education with a widespread advertising campaign to "sell America."

Still, not all Americans favored America's entry into the war. German and Irish Americans tended to oppose the Allies. Opposition also came from **conscientious objectors**, people whose moral or religious beliefs forbade them to fight in wars.

During the war, the U.S. government restricted individual rights. In June 1917, Congress passed the Espionage Act, which banned subversive newspapers, magazines, or printed materials on the grounds that they were forms of **espionage**. Congress further limited freedom of speech with the Sedition Act. In *Schenck* v. *United States* (1919), the Supreme Court ruled that there are times when the First Amendment protections on speech do not apply.

The war also brought substantial social changes. It created jobs for women while men were serving in the military and ushered in the Nineteenth Amendment, which gave women the right to vote. Meanwhile, many African Americans from the rural South were moving to the industrial North. The Great Migration saw more than 1.2 million African Americans move to the North to escape racism and find better jobs. Many Mexicans also sought to improve their lives. Some crossed the border into the United States in search of jobs. World War I had opened up new opportunities for women, African Americans, and Mexican Americans.

Lesson Vocabulary

conscientious objectors person whose moral or religious beliefs forbid him or her to fight in wars

espionage disloyal or treasonable activities

Name _____ Class _____ Date _____

TOPIC 12 LESSON 3
Lesson Summary
THE END OF WORLD WAR I

MODIFIED CORNELL NOTES

When the United States entered World War I in 1917, the conflict had become a deadly stalemate. Hoping to end the conflict before the Americans could make a difference, Germany renewed unrestricted submarine warfare. British and American convoys provided mutual safety by sending warships to protect merchant ships. As a result, shipping losses from U-boat attacks fell sharply.

In November 1917, radical communists led by Vladimir Lenin gained control of Russia. Fighting stopped between Russia and Germany, which allowed Germany to launch an all-out offensive on the Western Front. American troops under the command of John J. Pershing helped stop the German offensive and launch successful counterattacks. On November 11, 1918, Germany surrendered, officially ending World War I.

In what became known as the Fourteen Points, President Woodrow Wilson promoted openness, encouraged independence, and supported freedom. Wilson also advocated **self-determination**, or the right of people to choose their own form of government. Finally, he asked to form the League of Nations, a world organization where countries could gather and peacefully resolve their quarrels.

In 1919, the victorious Allies held a peace conference in France. Although Wilson's hope for the League of Nations was fulfilled, the various peace treaties created almost as many problems as they solved. The other Allied leaders insisted that Germany make **reparations**, or payment for war damages. When the map of Europe was redrawn, national self-determination was violated many times.

In the United States, many people opposed the treaty. A handful of senators known as the **"irreconcilables"** believed that the United States should not entangle itself in world organizations such as the League of Nations. A larger group of senators, led by Henry Cabot Lodge and known as **"reservationists,"** opposed the treaty as it was written. Wilson and his opponents refused to put aside their differences and compromise, and the Senate did not ratify the treaty. Without full American support, the League of Nations proved unable to maintain peace among nations.

Lesson Vocabulary

self-determination the right of people to choose their own form of government

reparations payment for war damages

"irreconcilables" isolationist senators who oppose any treaty ending World War I that had a League of Nations folded into it

"reservationists" group of U.S. senators who were prepared to vote for the Treaty of Versailles as long as some changes were made to it

Copyright © by Pearson Education, Inc., or its affiliates. All Rights Reserved.

Name _____ Class _____ Date _____

TOPIC 12 LESSON 4

Lesson Summary
THE POSTWAR ECONOMY BOOMS

MODIFIED CORNELL NOTES

The end of the war meant the end of wartime economic opportunities for women and African Americans. Adding to this crisis atmosphere were normal postwar adjustments. Falling agricultural prices made it difficult for farmers to pay their debts. **Inflation**, or rising prices, meant industrial workers' wages did not buy as much as they had bought during the war.

By 1920, the United States was the richest, most industrialized country in the world. The United States was also the largest **creditor nation** in the world, meaning that other countries owed the United States more money than the United States owed them. As a result of World War I, America's economic and political standing in the world had fundamentally changed.

During the 1920s, revolutionary **mass-production** techniques enabled American workers to produce more goods in less time. Because of this, the economy boomed. The automobile industry played a major role in the boom. Carmaker Henry Ford introduced new methods and ideas that changed the way manufactured goods were made. Ford also hired **scientific management** experts to improve his **assembly line** for the mass production of automobiles. In two years, the time it took to build an automobile dropped from more than 12 hours to just 90 minutes. This made the Model T affordable for most Americans, and automobile ownership skyrocketed.

(Continues on the next page.)

Lesson Vocabulary

inflation   rising prices

creditor nation   country which is owed more money by other countries than it owes other countries

mass-production   production of goods in large numbers through the use of machinery and assembly lines

scientific management   theory of management that studies how work is done with the goal of improving efficiency

assembly line   arrangement of equipment and workers in which work passes from operation to operation in direct line until the product is assembled

Copyright © by Pearson Education, Inc., or its affiliates. All Rights Reserved.

Name _____ Class _____ Date _____

TOPIC 12 LESSON 4
Lesson Summary
THE POSTWAR ECONOMY BOOMS (continued)

MODIFIED CORNELL NOTES

A flood of new, affordable goods became available to the public, creating a **consumer revolution**. At the same time, a new kind of credit called **installment buying** enabled consumers to buy goods they otherwise could not have afforded. Buyers made a small down payment on a product and paid the rest in monthly installments.

Americans were also buying stock on credit. As stock prices soared in a **bull market**, people began **buying on margin**, paying as little as 10 percent of the stock price upfront to a broker. If the stock price rose, the buyer could pay off the broker and still make a profit. If the price fell, the buyer still owed the broker the full price of the stock.

The economic boom was felt more in cities, where jobs were plentiful, than in rural areas. As cities grew, people moved out to suburbs and drove their new automobiles into the city to work.

Lesson Vocabulary

consumer revolution   flood of new, affordable goods in the decades after World War I

installment buying   method of purchase in which buyer makes a small down payment and then pays off the rest of the debt in regular monthly payments

bull market   period of rising stock prices

buying on margin   system of buying stocks in which a buyer pays a small percentage of the purchase price while the broker advances the rest

Name _____ Class _____ Date _____

TOPIC 12 LESSON 5
Lesson Summary
GOVERNMENT IN THE 1920s

MODIFIED CORNELL NOTES

In 1920, fun-loving Warren G. Harding was elected President. Preferring a laissez-faire approach to business, Harding named banker Andrew Mellon as Secretary of the Treasury. Together they worked to reduce regulations on businesses and to raise protective tariff rates. This made it easier for U.S. producers to sell goods at home. In response, Europeans also raised tariffs, making U.S. products more expensive there. Laws had been previously passed to break up monopolies and protect workers, but Harding favored less restriction on businesses. Secretary of Commerce Herbert Hoover asked business leaders to voluntarily make advancements.

Harding admitted that he preferred playing golf or poker to governing. He trusted his friends with important government positions. One friend, Charles Forbes, wasted millions of dollars while running the Veterans' Bureau. Another, Secretary of the Interior Albert Fall, created the biggest **scandal** of Harding's administration. In the Teapot Dome scandal, Fall took **bribes** to transfer control of oil reserves from the United States Navy to private oilmen. Fall was later forced to return the oil and sentenced to a year in jail. Harding died in 1923, before the full extent of the scandal came to light.

The new President, Calvin Coolidge, was quiet and honest. He put his administration in the hands of men who held to the simple **virtues** of an older generation. Like Harding, he mistrusted the use of legislation to achieve social change. He favored big business. He reduced the national debt and lowered taxes to give incentives to businesses. However, Coolidge said and did nothing about many of the country's problems, such as low prices for farm crops, racial discrimination, and low wages.

In foreign policy, Coolidge pushed European governments to repay war debts to the United States. In 1924, an agreement known as the Dawes Plan was arranged to help Germany, France, and Great Britain repay those debts. In 1928, exhausted by World War I, 62 nations signed the Kellogg-Briand Pact, a treaty that outlawed war. Unfortunately, there was no way for nations to enforce the treaty, and it was quickly forgotten.

Lesson Vocabulary

scandal an event involving immoral or illegal behavior that shocks and upsets the public

bribe money or valuables given to someone to influence behavior, often illegally or unethically

virtue a moral quality

Copyright © by Pearson Education, Inc., or its affiliates. All Rights Reserved.

Name _____ Class _____ Date _____

TOPIC 12
LESSON 6

Lesson Summary

AN UNSETTLED SOCIETY

MODIFIED CORNELL NOTES

As the 1920s began, striking differences arose between urban and rural America. Urban Americans enjoyed a rising standard of living and embraced a modern view of the world. City dwellers tended to value education and to be advocates of science and social change.

By contrast, times were hard in rural America. Formal education was considered less important than keeping the farm going. People tended to be conservative about political and social issues, preferring to keep things the way they were. Many rural Americans believed that the Bible was literally true. This belief was called **fundamentalism**. It opposed **modernism**, which stressed science.

The emergence of the Soviet Union as a communist nation compounded the fear of radicals and communists. Communist ideology called for an international workers' revolution, and communist revolts in central and eastern Europe made it seem like the worldwide revolution was starting.

Widespread fear of suspected communists and radicals thought to be plotting revolution within the United States prompted the first American Red Scare. In early 1920, Attorney General A. Mitchell Palmer mounted a series of raids, known as the Palmer Raids. Police arrested thousands of people, some who were radicals and some who were simply immigrants from southern or eastern Europe. To many, these actions seemed to attack the liberties that Americans held most dear.

A wave of immigration inspired nativist politicians to pass laws creating a **quota system** and forcing immigrants to pass a literacy test. The quota system set limits on the number of new immigrants allowed into the United States. Although many Americans appreciated the nation's growing diversity, many did not. In 1915, the Ku Klux Klan was reorganized in Georgia. This violent group, whose leaders had titles such as Grand Dragon and Imperial Wizard, promoted hatred of African Americans, Jews, Catholics, and immigrants.

Another divisive issue of the 1920s was Prohibition. In 1919 the states ratified the Eighteenth Amendment to the United States Constitution, which forbade the manufacture, distribution, and sale (but not consumption) of alcohol. Congress then passed the Volstead Act to enforce the amendment. Police often turned a blind eye to illegal drinking establishments, which left room for **bootleggers** not only to sell alcohol but also to expand into other illegal activities, such as prostitution, drugs, robbery, and murder. Thus, Prohibition unintentionally led to the growth of organized crime.

Lesson Vocabulary

fundamentalism   movement or attitude stressing strict and literal adherence to a set of basic religious principles

modernism   artistic and literary movement sparked by a break with past conventions

quota system   arrangement that limited the number of immigrants who could enter the United States from specific countries

bootlegger   one who sells illegal alcohol

Name _____ Class _____ Date _____

Topic 12 Lesson 7: Lesson Summary
THE ROARING TWENTIES

MODIFIED CORNELL NOTES

As urban Americans' wages rose in the 1920s, workers also enjoyed shorter workweeks. For the first time, a large city-dwelling population had free time and money to spend on entertainment. Movies were one of the most popular forms of entertainment and were attended by 60 to 100 million Americans each week. Actors such as comedian Charlie Chaplin, heartthrob Rudolf Valentino, and cowboy William S. Hart became silent film stars. Then, in 1927, the movie The Jazz Singer startled audiences when Al Jolson said, "You ain't seen nothin' yet." The Jazz Singer became the first movie to include sound matched to the action on the screen, and the era of "talkies" was born.

For entertainment at home, Americans bought millions of phonographs and radios. By 1923, almost 600 licensed radio stations broadcast to more than 600,000 radio sets. Americans across the continent listened to the same songs, learned the same dances, and shared a popular culture as never before. People admired the same heroes, such as Babe Ruth, the home-run king, and aviator Charles Lindbergh, who was the first to fly solo across the Atlantic Ocean.

American women challenged political, economic, social, and educational boundaries. With passage of the Nineteenth Amendment, they won the right to vote. Many ran for political office and more joined the workforce. Some women, known as **flappers**, shocked society by wearing short skirts and bobbed hair. At home, new electric appliances made housework easier. Popular magazines, **sociological studies**, novels, and movies all featured the "New Woman" of the 1920s prominently.

A spirit of modernism grew, especially in cities. Austrian psychologist Sigmund Freud contributed to modernism with his theory that human behavior is driven by unconscious desire rather than by rational thought. Painters rejected artistic norms. Writers, including F. Scott Fitzgerald and Ernest Hemingway, wrote about the meaning of life and war. Their literary masterpieces examined **subconscious** desires and the dark side of the American dream.

Lesson Vocabulary

flapper   young woman from the 1920s who defied traditional rules of conduct and dress

sociological study   research into the workings of society, social institutions, and social relationships

subconscious   something that exists in people's minds but is not necessarily known or felt

TOPIC 12, LESSON 8

Lesson Summary
THE HARLEM RENAISSANCE

Millions of African Americans left the South after World War I to find racial equity and economic opportunity in the North. In the South, they faced low-paying jobs, substandard schools, Jim Crow oppression, and the threat of lynching. However, they found well-paying jobs, middle-class communities of African American professionals, and a growing political voice in cities such as New York, Chicago, and Detroit.

Harlem in New York City became a **haven** for about 200,000 African Americans from the South as well as black immigrants from the Caribbean. One immigrant was Marcus Garvey, a Jamaican who had traveled widely. After seeing that blacks were treated poorly, Garvey organized a "Back to Africa" movement that urged black unity and separation of the races.

It was F. Scott Fitzgerald who called the 1920s the "Jazz Age." However, it was African Americans who gave the age its **jazz**. A truly **indigenous** American musical form, jazz emerged in the South as a combination of African American and European musical styles. African Americans migrating north brought the new musical style with them. Musicians such as trumpet player Louis Armstrong took jazz to the world. Singer Bessie Smith, nicknamed the "Empress of the Blues," was very popular and became the highest-paid African American entertainer of the 1920s.

The decade also saw the Harlem Renaissance, an outpouring of art and literature that explored the African American experience. Among its most famous writers was Jamaican-born Claude McKay, whose novels and poems were militant calls for action. Langston Hughes celebrated African American culture, and Zora Neale Hurston wrote about women's desire for independence.

The Great Depression ended the Harlem Renaissance. However, the pride and unity it created provided a foundation for the future civil rights movement.

Lesson Vocabulary

haven   a place that offers security and opportunities
jazz   a musical form based on improvisation
indigenous   original or native to a country or region

MODIFIED CORNELL NOTES

Name _____ Class _____ Date _____

TOPIC 12: Review Questions
WORLD WAR I AND THE 1920s

Answer the questions below using the information in the Lesson Summaries on the previous pages.

Lesson 1: America Enters World War I

1. Why did the United States get involved in the war?
_____
_____

2. Identify Causes Identify the causes of World War I.
_____
_____

Lesson 2: The Home Front During World War I

3. Why did conscientious objectors oppose the war?
_____
_____

4. Summarize Summarize how the American government mobilized the public to support the war effort.
_____
_____

Lesson 3 The End of World War I

5. Describe the aims of the Fourteen Points.
_____
_____

6. Identify Supporting Details Sequence the events that led the U.S. Senate to not ratify the treaty ending World War I.
_____
_____

Lesson 4: The Postwar Economy Booms

7. How did mass production influence the economy?
_____
_____

8. How did the consumer revolution lead to new ways of purchasing items?
_____
_____

Copyright © by Pearson Education, Inc., or its affiliates. All Rights Reserved.

Name _____ Class _____ Date _____

TOPIC 12: Review Questions
WORLD WAR I AND THE 1920s (continued)

Lesson 5: Government in the 1920s
9. What was the Teapot Dome scandal?

10. **Compare and Contrast** How did the differences between Presidents Harding and Coolidge influence their presidencies?

Lesson 6: An Unsettled Society
11. What did the Eighteenth Amendment forbid?

12. **Contrast** Select an issue that divided Americans. Contrast the ways rural and urban Americans felt about this issue.

Lesson 7: The Roaring Twenties
13. What technological advances led to cultural change during the 1920s?

14. **Summarize** List three ways American culture changed in the 1920s.

Lesson 8: The Harlem Renaissance
15. Why did many African Americans migrate north?

16. **Identify Main Ideas** What was the Harlem Renaissance?

Name _____ Class _____ Date _____

TOPIC 13
Note Taking Study Guide
THE GREAT DEPRESSION AND THE NEW DEAL

Focus Question: What were the goals of the New Deal and what programs were created to achieve those goals?

As you read, note specific examples of goals and programs and list them in the appropriate column.

The New Deal	
Goals	**Programs**

Copyright © by pearson Education, Inc., or its affiliates. All Rights Reserved.

118

Name _____ Class _____ Date _____

TOPIC 13 LESSON 1

Lesson Summary
CAUSES OF THE DEPRESSION

MODIFIED CORNELL NOTES

The Roaring Twenties were a Republican decade. Beginning in 1920, Republican Presidents led the nation and took credit for the good economic times. In 1928, the country continued to support the Republicans by electing Herbert Hoover as President. However, the nation's prosperity was not as deep or as sturdy as it appeared.

American farmers faced difficult times in the 1920s. They had borrowed money to buy land and machinery to increase the harvest yields during World War I. Although the demand for American crops fell after the war, farmers were still producing large harvests. Cheap food flooded the markets, lowering farmers' profits and making debt repayment hard.

Industrial workers, whose wages rose steadily, did better than farmers. The owners of companies did even better. They became very rich. In fact, in 1929, the wealthiest 0.1 percent of the population earned about the same amount of money (bottom 42 percent combined). However, the people with great wealth could not buy enough goods to keep the economy strong. Still, many workers took advantage of **easy credit** to buy products. This disguised the problem and helped grow the economy.

By 1929, it became clear that too much money was being poured into stock **speculation**. Investors often borrowed money to buy stocks, then sold them to turn a quick profit. Frantic buying and selling inflated the prices of stocks to unrealistic levels. Finally, all the problems began to converge. A sharp drop in stock prices led to panicked selling. Stock prices bottomed out and destroyed whole fortunes in hours on Black Tuesday, October 29, 1929.

The stock market crash marked the beginning of the Great Depression, a period lasting from 1929 to 1941 in which the U.S. economy faltered and unemployment soared. Thousands of banks closed and many businesses failed. The government tried to boost the sale of American goods by passing the Hawley-Smoot Tariff, which placed high taxes on foreign goods. The result was closed markets and unsold goods, which destroyed international trade. Economists still disagree on what was the most important factor leading to the Great Depression, which eventually affected the whole world.

Lesson Vocabulary

easy credit   loan obtained from a lender willing to lend money to a borrower without checking thoroughly that the borrower has the financial ability to repay the loan

speculation   practice of making high-risk investments in hopes of obtaining large profits

Copyright © by Pearson Education, Inc., or its affiliates. All Rights Reserved.

Name _____ Class _____ Date _____

TOPIC 13 LESSON 2

Lesson Summary
AMERICANS SUFFER

MODIFIED CORNELL NOTES

The Great Depression deeply affected Americans. Some lost everything they had while others struggled simply to survive. In the cities, Americans faced rampant unemployment. Between 1921 and 1929, annual average unemployment rates never rose above 3.7 percent. By 1933, almost 25 percent of workers were without jobs. As unemployed families ran out of money, their hardship deepened. Drastic necessity forced them to sell their belongings. Sometimes a family's only food came from a **bread line**, where people lined up for handouts from charities or public agencies. Many people were evicted from their homes. With no place else to go, they sometimes grouped together in Hoovervilles—makeshift shantytowns of tents and shacks built on public land or vacant lots.

Conditions were bad in rural America, too. Before the depression, farmers had already been struggling. During the depression, their problems worsened. Crop prices dropped lower. Between 1930 and 1934, nearly one million farmers lost their homes for failure to pay their mortgages. Some farmers stayed on the land as **tenant farmers**, working for bigger landowners rather than for themselves. A severe drought and overfarming on the Great Plains turned the soil to dust, making farming impossible and creating huge dust storms. High plains regions in Texas, Oklahoma, Kansas, New Mexico, and Colorado became known as the Dust Bowl. Many farmers left the area and moved to California to look for work. Because some of these people were from Oklahoma, Dust Bowl refugees became known as Okies.

Minorities were hit the hardest by the depression. African American sharecroppers were thrown off the land they had farmed and migrated north. In 1932, unemployment among African Americans was nearly double the national rate. In the Southwest, many white Americans urged **repatriation** of Mexican Americans. Repatriation involved government efforts to send Mexican immigrants and their American children back to Mexico.

For many Americans, the Great Depression was a time of great hopelessness and despair.

Lesson Vocabulary

bread line   line of people waiting for food handouts from charities or public agencies

tenant farmer   farmer who pays rent to a landowner for the use of the land

repatriation   process by which government officials return persons to their country of origin

Name _____ Class _____ Date _____

Topic 13 Lesson 3: Lesson Summary — TWO PRESIDENTS RESPOND

MODIFIED CORNELL NOTES

From big cities to small towns, the Great Depression spread misery across America. As the crisis deepened, Herbert Hoover struggled to respond to the nation's problems.

At first, Hoover felt that government should not interfere with what he thought was the natural downswing of the business cycle.

Next, Hoover called for a policy of **localism**. This policy asked state and local government to provide more jobs and relief measures. However, businesses cut wages and laid off workers, towns and states did not have the resources to respond to the crisis, and charities ran low on money.

Finally, the President decided to adopt a policy of **trickle-down economics**. The idea was that the government would provide loans to bankers, and in turn, they could lend money to businesses. Businesses would then hire workers, leading to increased production and consumption as well as the end of the depression. At Hoover's urging, Congress created the Reconstruction Finance Corporation (RFC) to provide loans to businesses. However, businesses did not always use them to hire workers.

Americans became increasingly unhappy with Hoover's handling of the depression. A group of almost 20,000 unemployed World War I veterans known as the Bonus Army marched in protest and set up camps in Washington, D.C. When riots broke out in July 1932, Hoover called in the military.

In November 1932, Franklin D. Roosevelt (FDR) won the presidency by more than 7 million votes.

In his first hundred days in office, FDR proposed and Congress passed 15 bills known as the first New Deal. These measures had three goals: relief, recovery, and reform.

(Continues on the next page.)

Lesson Vocabulary

localism policy relied on by President Hoover in the early years of the Great Depression, whereby local and state governments act as primary agents of economic relief

trickle-down economics economic theory that holds that financial benefits given to banks and large businesses will trickle down to smaller businesses and consumers

Name _____ Class _____ Date _____

TOPIC 13 LESSON 3

Lesson Summary
TWO PRESIDENTS RESPOND (continued)

MODIFIED CORNELL NOTES

Relief efforts included the establishment of the Tennessee Valley Authority (TVA), which built dams in the Tennessee River valley to control floods and generate electric power, and the creation of the Civilian Conservation Corps (CCC). The CCC provided jobs for more than 2 million young men. They replanted forests, built trails, dug irrigation ditches, and fought fires. Recovery efforts included the National Recovery Administration (NRA) and the Public Works Administration (PWA). The NRA developed industry codes that set **minimum wages** for workers and **minimum prices** for goods. The PWA created millions of new jobs constructing bridges, dams, power plants, and government buildings. Additionally, FDR sought to reform the nation's financial institutions. The Federal Deposit Insurance Corporation (FDIC) insured bank deposits, and the Securities Exchange Commission (SEC) regulated the stock market.

Some Americans thought the New Deal made the government too powerful. Others thought that the New Deal did not provide enough help to citizens. The strongest criticism from this second group came from individuals with roots in the Populist movement.

Lesson Vocabulary

minimum wage   lowest wage allowed by law
minimum price   lowest price allowed by law

Copyright © by Pearson Education, Inc., or its affiliates. All Rights Reserved.

Name _____ Class _____ Date _____

Topic 13 Lesson 4
Lesson Summary
THE NEW DEAL EXPANDS

MODIFIED CORNELL NOTES

President Franklin D. Roosevelt's goals for the first New Deal were relief, recovery, and reform. He used legislation passed by the second New Deal to accomplish the goals of promoting the general welfare and protecting citizens' rights.

In the spring of 1935, Congress created the Works Progress Administration (WPA) to provide new jobs doing public works. The WPA even provided programs to employ displaced artists. The government paid for WPA programs by spending money it didn't have. British economist John Maynard Keynes argued that such **deficit spending** was needed to end the depression.

The Social Security Act created a pension system for retirees, unemployment insurance for workers who lost their jobs, and aid for people with disabilities. New programs aided farmers. The Rural Electrification Administration (REA) helped bring electricity to farms. New laws also aided industrial workers. The Wagner Act gave workers the right to **collective bargaining**. This meant that employers had to negotiate with unions about hours, wages, and other working conditions. The Fair Labor Standards Act of 1938 established a minimum wage and a maximum number of hours for the workweek. It also outlawed child labor.

During the Great Depression there was an upsurge in union activity. The Congress of Industrial Organization (CIO) was established to organize workers in major industries. In 1936, CIO members staged a **sit-down strike** against General Motors, refusing to leave the workplace until a settlement had been reached. Their success led to other strikes, which improved wages and working conditions for union members.

(Continues on the next page.)

Lesson Vocabulary

deficit spending   spending of public funds raised by borrowing

collective bargaining   process in which employers negotiate with labor unions about wages, hours, and other working conditions

sit-down strike   organized labor action in which workers stop working and occupy the workplace until their demands are met

TOPIC 13 LESSON 4

Section Summary
THE NEW DEAL EXPANDS (continued)

MODIFIED CORNELL NOTES

FDR faced challenges from the Supreme Court, which struck down a number of the key laws of the New Deal. To dilute the power of the sitting Justices, FDR asked Congress to add six new Justices to the nine-member court, a plan that became known as **court packing**. After 1937, the Supreme Court became more willing to accept New Deal legislation. After a new economic downturn in 1938, FDR chose not to try to force more reforms through Congress.

Lesson Vocabulary

court packing President Franklin D. Roosevelt's plan to add six new Justices to the nine-member Supreme Court after the Court had ruled some New Deal laws to be unconstitutional

Name _____ Class _____ Date _____

TOPIC 13 LESSON 5

Lesson Summary
EFFECTS OF THE NEW DEAL

MODIFIED CORNELL NOTES

The New Deal brought fundamental changes to the nation. Some women were provided with the opportunity to increase their political influence. Eleanor Roosevelt transformed the office of First Lady to a politically active position. She traveled extensively and advocated equal justice for all. The first female Cabinet member was Secretary of Labor Frances Perkins, who played a leading role in establishing Social Security and a minimum wage. Despite this, the New Deal did not fight to end gender discrimination in the workplace.

President Roosevelt invited African American leaders to advise him. These unofficial advisers became known as the Black Cabinet. One member, Mary McLeod Bethune, was a powerful champion of racial equality. Even so, racial discrimination and injustice continued to plague African Americans.

The Indian New Deal was a program to help American Indians by providing funding for the construction of new schools and hospitals. In 1934, the Indian Reorganization Act restored tribal control of American Indian lands. The Bureau of Indian Affairs also stopped discouraging the practice of traditional American Indian customs.

By his death in 1945, FDR had united a culturally diverse group of Americans into a strong political force called the New Deal coalition, which gave the Democratic Party a sizable majority in both houses of Congress. FDR and the New Deal also helped to unify the nation. Programs such as the WPA allowed people of varied backgrounds to get to know one another, breaking down regional and ethnic prejudices.

New Deal programs increased the size and scope of the federal government like never before. The government assumed responsibility for providing for the welfare of children as well as the poor, elderly, sick, disabled, and unemployed. This led to the rise of a **welfare state**.

The expanding role of the government, including the creation of many new federal agencies, gave the executive branch much more power. Roosevelt was elected President four times. After his death, there was a call for limiting the President's term of office. In 1951, the Twenty-second Amendment limited the President to two consecutive terms in office.

Lesson Vocabulary

welfare state   government that assumes responsibility for providing for the welfare of the poor, elderly, sick, and unemployed

MODIFIED CORNELL NOTES

Topic 13 Lesson 6 — Lesson Summary
CULTURE DURING THE DEPRESSION

Entertainment became big business during the 1930s, creating a golden age in American culture. Large radio networks dominated the airwaves, while a cluster of film companies ruled the silver screen. Radio ownership grew during the decade, and nearly two thirds of all Americans attended at least one movie a week.

The movies were a form of escapism during the Great Depression as Americans sought relief from their concerns. Movies like The Wizard of Oz promised weary audiences that their dreams really could come true. In the early 1930s, many films reflected the public's distrust of **big business** and government. Others, such as the films of Frank Capra, celebrated American idealism and the triumph of the common man over adversity.

Radio brought news and entertainment into American homes. FDR used fireside radio chats to explain his New Deal programs. National radio networks broadcasted dramas, comedies, soap operas, and variety shows. Episodes from *The Lone Ranger* began running in 1933 and lasted for more than 20 years. Sometimes the lines between news and entertainment were blurred. When the Mercury Theatre broadcasted a drama called *War of the Worlds* on October 30, 1938, many people panicked, believing that Martians were actually invading.

Music also provided a diversion from hard times, whether on the radio at home or in nightclubs. Americans enjoyed "swing" music played by "big bands." Blues singers focused on the harsh conditions faced by African Americans. Woody Guthrie wrote ballads about the Okies, farmers who fled the Dust Bowl.

The federal government funded the arts for the first time through programs such as the Federal Art Project. Artists painted huge **murals** on public buildings across the nation. Dorothea Lange and other photographers documented the plight of American farmers.

Many writers produced novels featuring working-class heroes. John Steinbeck's *The Grapes of Wrath* traces the fictional Joad family from the Oklahoma Dust Bowl to California. Lillian Hellman wrote several plays featuring strong roles for women as well as screenplays for movies. Americans also enjoyed comic strips and comic books.

Lesson Vocabulary

big business   large-scale businesses controlled by corporations

murals   large painting applied directly to a wall or a ceiling

Name _____ Class _____ Date _____

Topic 13: Review Questions
THE GREAT DEPRESSION AND THE NEW DEAL

Answer the questions below using the information in the Lesson Summaries on the previous pages.

Lesson 1: Causes of the Depression

1. In 1928, how did Americans show their approval for the way Republicans handled the economy?
   _____
   _____

2. **Cause and Effect** Select a cause of the Great Depression. Explain how it contributed to the depression.
   _____
   _____

Lesson 2: Americans Suffer

3. What was repatriation, and who was most affected by it?
   _____
   _____

4. **Categorize** What were some of the problems present in both urban and rural America?
   _____
   _____

Lesson 3 Two Presidents Respond

5. Name two New Deal policies that provided immediate relief to Americans.
   _____
   _____

6. **Identify Supporting Details** List the details that support the conclusion that Hoover's policy of volunteerism failed.
   _____
   _____

Lesson 4: The New Deal Expands

7. Explain how New Deal legislation promoted the well-being of workers.
   _____
   _____

TOPIC 13 Review Questions
THE GREAT DEPRESSION AND THE NEW DEAL (continued)

8. Connect Ideas How did the policies of the second New Deal improve the standard of living of Americans?

Lesson 5: Effects of the New Deal

9. How did the New Deal lead to the rise of a welfare state?

10. Identify Main Ideas How did the New Deal benefit different groups in American society?

Lesson 6 Culture During the Depression

11. Identify Main Ideas and Details In what ways were the 1930s a golden age for entertainment?

12. What was the Federal Art Project?

Name _____ Class _____ Date _____

TOPIC 14: Note Taking Study Guide
WORLD WAR II

Focus Question: In what ways did Americans contribute to their nation's war effort during World War II, and how did these contributions create new opportunities for certain groups of people in America who participated in the war?

As you read, note specific examples of contributions that different groups of people made. Write these in the empty spaces of the web that surround the central core labeled "Contributions."

Contributions

Copyright © by Pearson Education, Inc., or its affiliates. All Rights Reserved.

129

Name _____ Class _____ Date _____

Topic 14 Lesson 1
Lesson Summary
RISE OF AGGRESSIVE DICTATORS

MODIFIED CORNELL NOTES

In the 1920s, some nations moved toward democracy. Others moved toward repressive dictatorships and **totalitarianism**, a type of government in which a single party or leader controls the economic, social, and cultural lives of a nation's people.

The 1917 communist revolution in the Soviet Union produced the first totalitarian state, headed by Vladimir Lenin. In 1924, Joseph Stalin took his place as the Communist Party's head.

A postwar economic depression troubled Italy. In 1922, the king asked the founder of the Fascist Party, Benito Mussolini, to form a government. Mussolini turned Italy into a fascist country with a controlled press, secret police, and no political parties.

Following World War I, Germany became a democracy. However, the Great Depression caused severe economic troubles in the 1930s. The National Socialist German Workers' Party (Nazi Party) led by Adolf Hitler rose to power. Hitler criticized many people, political programs, and ideologies, but his sharpest assaults were against communists and Jews. Hitler was violently **anti-Semitic**, or prejudiced against Jewish people. He was appointed to chancellor in 1933 and became president of Germany within two years.

In Japan, the Great Depression ended a period of increased democracy and peaceful change. Military leaders argued that expansion throughout Asia would solve Japan's problems. Japan attacked Manchuria and established a puppet state in 1931. Six years later, Japan attacked China again, raiding the capital city with such brutality that it became known as the "Rape of Nanjing."

In the 1930s, Italy and Germany resorted to acts of aggression similar to those of Japan in Asia. Hitler reclaimed the Saar region from French control and sent troops into the Rhineland, while Mussolini led an invasion into Ethiopia. The League of Nations did almost nothing to stop aggression.

France, Britain, and the United States pursued the policy of **appeasement** toward the fascist leaders. Appeasement means granting concessions to a potential enemy to maintain peace. However, this approach only encouraged the leaders to become bolder and more aggressive.

Lesson Vocabulary

totalitarianism a theory of government in which a single party or leader controls the economic, social, and cultural lives of its people

anti-Semitic prejudiced against Jewish people

appeasement policy of granting concessions in order to keep peace

TOPIC 14 LESSON 2

Lesson Summary
AMERICA DEBATES INVOLVEMENT

MODIFIED CORNELL NOTES

After Japan's violent attack on China in 1937, President Roosevelt criticized the Japanese aggression. The United States, however, continued to back away from intervention in foreign conflicts.

Despite a military alliance among France, Britain, and Poland, Germany invaded Poland in 1939. Britain and France declared war on Germany, and World War II had begun. The Axis Powers would come to include Germany, Italy, Japan, and several other nations. The Axis Powers fought the Allies, which included Britain, France, and eventually the Soviet Union, China, and the United States.

Germany used a new technique called **blitzkrieg**, or "lightning war." Tanks and planes attacked in a coordinated effort and quickly conquered Poland. In April 1940, Denmark and Norway fell to the German blitzkrieg. In May, Germany took the Netherlands, Belgium, and Luxembourg, and then invaded France. The next month, Germany attacked Britain from the air.

Winston Churchill, the prime minister of Britain, hoped to convince the United States to join the Allies. Accounts by news reporter Edward R. Murrow on the bombing of London shocked the American public. Murrow emphasized that the Germans were bombing civilians, not armies or military sites. Despite its isolationist policies, the United States moved slowly toward involvement. Congress passed the Neutrality Act of 1939. This law helped the Allies buy goods and munitions from the United States. Isolationists, however, believed that getting involved in a bloody European war would be wasteful and dangerous.

Even though most Americans wanted to remain **neutral**, President Roosevelt constantly argued for helping Britain. In early 1941, Congress approved the Lend-Lease Act. This act gave the President the power to sell, give, or lease weapons to protect the United States. In 1941, Roosevelt also met with Churchill to discuss the war. They signed the Atlantic Charter, a document that endorsed national self-determination and an international system of "general security." The agreement signaled the deepening alliance between the two nations. Hitler was not blind to American support of the Allies. In the fall of 1941, he ordered German U-boats to attack American ships. U.S. involvement in the war seemed inevitable.

Lesson Vocabulary

blitzkrieg "lightning war" that emphasized the use of speed and firepower to penetrate deep into the enemy's territory

neutral not supporting any side in a war

Name _____ Class _____ Date _____

TOPIC 14 LESSON 3

Lesson Summary
AMERICA ENTERS WORLD WAR II

MODIFIED CORNELL NOTES

As Japan expanded its empire throughout Asia, its relationship with the United States worsened. Japan needed resources such as oil, steel, and rubber to maintain its military. The United States began to withhold these goods to limit Japan's expansion. The United States also instituted a **trade embargo** against Japan.

At first, Hideki Tojo, the Japanese prime minister, tried to keep the United States neutral. However, when a trade agreement with the United States failed, Tojo decided on a decisive military strike. On December 7, 1941, hundreds of Japanese airplanes bombed the site of the United States Navy's main base in the Pacific at Pearl Harbor, Hawaii. Nearly 2,500 people were killed in this devastating surprise attack. Many ships were sunk, and hundreds of aircraft were destroyed or damaged.

Congress immediately declared war on Japan. Germany and Italy then declared war on the United States. George Marshall, United States Army chief of staff, triggered plans for building up the military as quickly as possible. Meanwhile, men from all ethnic and racial backgrounds joined branches of the military by the millions. Thousands of women joined the Women's Army Corps (WAC) as clerical workers, truck drivers, instructors, and lab technicians. The government also created agencies to ensure the production of supplies needed for the military. These agencies allocated scarce materials to the proper industries. Private companies developed innovative production techniques to make huge quantities of war goods, creating a production miracle that was key to helping the Allies fight the war.

In Asia, United States Army General Douglas MacArthur struggled unsuccessfully to hold the Philippines against the Japanese forces. U.S. forces had to retreat, and MacArthur evacuated to Australia in March. Some 70,000 U.S. and Filipino troops fell back to the Bataan Peninsula and the citadel on Corregidor Island, where they lived on half and quarter rations. In April 1942, the soldiers on the Bataan Peninsula surrendered. Japanese troops forced these sick and malnourished men to march many miles. More than 7,000 American and Filipino troops died on the march, which is known as the Bataan Death March. Finally, in May 1942, the **citadel** on Corregidor Island surrendered, leaving Japan in control of the Philippines.

By the summer of 1942, Japan controlled most of Southeast Asia and the western Pacific. Then in May 1942, the United States Navy finally began to stop the Japanese advance. At the Battle of Coral Sea, the United States Navy prevented Japan from taking a key spot in New Guinea. The Japanese offensive was over.

Lesson Vocabulary

trade embargo   prohibition of trade with a particular country
citadel   fortress

Copyright © by Pearson Education, Inc., or its affiliates. All Rights Reserved.

Name _____ Class _____ Date _____

TOPIC 14 LESSON 4

Lesson Summary
A WAR ON TWO FRONTS

MODIFIED CORNELL NOTES

The attack on Pearl Harbor brought the United States into World War II. The Allies' ultimate goal was to fight and win a two-front war. Their first objective, however, was to defeat Hitler. The United States was producing millions of tons of guns, tanks, and other supplies. German U-boats, however, had sunk over 3,500 merchant ships bound for Britain. By mid-1943, using radar, bombers, and underwater depth charges, Allied forces were sinking U-boats faster than Germany could manufacture them. The Allies had begun to win the war in the North Atlantic.

In 1941, Germany attacked Russia, and Stalin wanted Roosevelt and Churchill to open a second front in France. In early 1942, British planes instead began **saturation bombing**, dropping large numbers of bombs on German cities. American bombers used **strategic bombing**, targeting key political and industrial centers. The Tuskegee Airmen, an African American fighter squadron, played a key role in the bombing campaign. In January 1943, after the long, bitter Battle of Stalingrad, the Russians turned back the German invasion of their country. During the same month, FDR announced that only the **unconditional surrender** of the Axis Powers would end the war. That is, they had to give up completely.

To help pave the way for an invasion of Italy, the Allies decided to push the Germans out of North Africa, where they had been fighting British troops since 1940. In February 1942, American General Dwight Eisenhower commanded the Allied invasion. After difficult battles, General George S. Patton, Jr. took charge of American forces. In May 1943, German and Italian forces in North Africa surrendered. Two months later, Allied forces invaded Sicily, two miles off the mainland of Italy. From there, they launched their invasion of Italy, and in September, Italy surrendered.

In spite of its "Europe first" strategy, the United States did not ignore the Pacific where Japanese forces had continued to advance. In June 1942, the Japanese attacked Midway, a vital American naval base in the central Pacific. The American naval commander, Admiral Chester Nimitz, had learned of the Japanese plans, and the Battle of Midway was a decisive American victory. It ended Japanese expansion in the Pacific and put Japan on the defensive.

Lesson Vocabulary

saturation bombing   tactic of dropping massive amounts of bombs in order to inflict maximum damage

strategic bombing   tactic of dropping bombs on key political and industrial targets

unconditional surrender   giving up completely without any concessions

TOPIC 14 LESSON 5

Lesson Summary

THE HOME FRONT

MODIFIED CORNELL NOTES

World War II fears and tensions tested civil liberties, but the war also provided new opportunities for women and minorities. Many women found jobs, especially in heavy industry. They gained confidence, knowledge, organizational experience, and a paycheck. However, few African Americans found meaningful employment with defense employers. In response, African American labor leader A. Philip Randolph planned a massive march on Washington, D.C., to protest employment discrimination. Under pressure, FDR issued Executive Order 8802. It assured fair hiring practices in any job funded with government money.

Wartime needs encouraged people to move to the South and Southwest to find jobs in defense industries. To alleviate the rural population drain, the United States initiated the *bracero* program. This program brought Mexican laborers to work on farms in the United States. Although they often faced discrimination, braceros contributed greatly to the war effort.

After the attack on Pearl Harbor, the federal government moved about 100,000 Japanese Americans living on the West Coast to camps in isolated locations under a policy of **internment**. There, they were held in jail-like conditions for the duration of the war. Some Japanese Americans went to court to seek their rights. In the 1944 case of *Korematsu* v. *United States*, the Supreme Court upheld the government's wartime internment policy. When the government lifted a ban on Japanese Americans serving in the armed forces, many enlisted. The Japanese American 442nd Regimental Combat Team fought in the Italian campaign and became the most decorated military unit in American history.

The war cost the United States $330 billion. To help pay for it, Congress levied a tax on all working Americans. **Rationing** was instituted to ensure that there would be adequate raw materials, such as oil and rubber, for war production. The federal Office of War Information (OWI) worked with the media to encourage support of the war effort. Millions of Americans bought war bonds and contributed to the war effort in many other ways, large and small.

Lesson Vocabulary

internment temporary imprisonment of members of a specific group

rationing government-controlled limits on the amount of certain goods that civilians could buy during wartime

Name _____ Class _____ Date _____

TOPIC 14 LESSON 6
Lesson Summary
THE ALLIES WIN WORLD WAR II

MODIFIED CORNELL NOTES

In 1943, the Allied leaders agreed to open a second front in France. On June 6, 1944, known as D-Day, British and American forces traveled across the English Channel to invade France from the west. More than 11,000 planes prepared the way, followed by more than 4,400 ships and landing crafts. By the end of the day, they had gained a toehold in France. On July 1, more than one million Allied troops had landed.

Germany now faced a hopeless two-front war because the Soviets were advancing from the east. In December 1944, Hitler ordered a counterattack, known as the Battle of the Bulge. Hitler's scenario called for German forces to capture communication and transportation hubs. The attack almost succeeded. However, with help from their bombers, the Allies managed to push the Germans out of France. By January 1945, the Soviet Army had reached the Oder River outside Berlin, and in April, the United States Army was just 50 miles west of Berlin. Hitler committed suicide on April 30, and on May 7, Germany surrendered.

American forces in the Pacific followed an **island-hopping** strategy in a steady path toward Japan. Japanese troops fought hard, and Japanese **kamikaze** pilots deliberately crashed their planes into American ships. By April 1945, American pilots finally made their way to Okinawa, 340 miles from Japan. From Okinawa, American pilots could bomb the Japanese home islands. American bombers hit factories, military bases, and cities.

Advances in technology helped determine the final outcome of the war. Albert Einstein, a famous scientist, had alerted FDR of the need to proceed with atomic development. Physicist J. Robert Oppenheimer was in charge of the scientific aspect of the program, known as the Manhattan Project. On the morning of July 16, 1945, the first atomic bomb was tested. In order to save American lives and to end the war, President Harry S. Truman decided to use the atomic bomb against Japan. On August 6, 1945, U.S. pilots dropped at atomic bomb on Hiroshima. Three days later, the United States dropped a second atomic bomb on Nagasaki. Emperor Hirohito made the decision to surrender, and on August 15, the Allies celebrated V-J (Victory in Japan) Day. World War II had been the most costly war in history. As many as 60 million people—mostly civilians—had died in the conflict.

Lesson Vocabulary

island-hopping World War II strategy that involved seizing selected Japanese-held islands in the Pacific while bypassing others

kamikaze Japanese pilots who deliberately crashed planes into American ships during World War II

Copyright © by Pearson Education, Inc., or its affiliates. All Rights Reserved.

Name _____ Class _____ Date _____

TOPIC 14 LESSON 7

Lesson Summary
THE HOLOCAUST

MODIFIED CORNELL NOTES

In 1945, there was no word for the Holocaust, the most horrific event of World War II. It was the Nazi attempt to kill all Jews, as well as other "undesirables," under their control. This was part of a racist Nazi ideology that considered Aryans—white northern European gentiles—superior to other people.

Hitler began to persecute the Jews as soon as he came to power. In 1935, the Nuremberg Laws denied citizenship to Jews and segregated them at every level of society. Acts of violence against Jews were common. The most serious occurred on November 9, 1938, and is called Kristallnacht, the "Night of Broken Glass." Secret police and military units destroyed more than 200 synagogues and 7,500 Jewish businesses, killed more than 200 Jews, and injured more than 600 others.

Hitler's "Final Solution to the Jewish question" was **genocide**, the willful annihilation of all Jews living in regions under his control. Jews and other "undesirables" were confined in **concentration camps**. In theory, the camps were designed to turn prisoners into "useful members" of the Third Reich. However, there were no restraints on guards, who tortured and killed prisoners without fear of reprisals. Doctors conducted experiments that killed prisoners or left them deformed. Many concentration camps were **death camps**, where prisoners were systematically exterminated. The largest death camp was Auschwitz in southern Poland.

Before the war, the United States and other countries could have done more if they had relaxed immigration policies and accepted more Jewish refugees. Once the war started, news of the mass killings began to filter to the West. In early 1944, FDR began to respond and established the War Refugee Board, which worked with the Red Cross to save thousands of Eastern European Jews. The enormity of the Nazi crime became real for most Americans only when Allied soldiers began to liberate the concentration camps. The revelation of the Holocaust increased American support for a Jewish homeland. Therefore, when Jewish settlers in Palestine proclaimed the state of Israel, President Truman immediately recognized the new nation.

Lesson Vocabulary

genocide willful annihilation of a racial, political, or cultural group

concentration camps camps used by the Nazis to imprison "undesirable" members of society

death camps Nazi camps designed for the extermination of prisoners

Name _____ Class _____ Date _____

TOPIC 14 LESSON 8

Lesson Summary
IMPACT OF WORLD WAR II

MODIFIED CORNELL NOTES

As World War II drew to an end, Japan and Germany kept fighting long after their defeat was certain. The protracted fighting gave the Allies time to make plans for a postwar world. In February 1945, Roosevelt, Churchill, and Stalin met at Yalta on the Black Sea. At the Yalta Conference, they discussed final strategy and crucial questions concerning postwar Germany, Eastern Europe, and Asia. A few months later, the Big Three, now composed of Stalin, Truman, and Attlee, met at Potsdam to formalize the decision to divide Germany into four zones of occupation. The war ended Western European domination of the world. Two **superpowers**—the United States and the Soviet Union—became the predominant nations of the postwar world.

Not all the changes that took place after the war ended were what the Allies had envisioned at Yalta and Potsdam. Communist and anticommunist interests clashed in Eastern Europe. Civil war resumed in China. Under American military occupation, Japan gained a new constitution that abolished the armed forces and enacted democratic reforms.

The United States, where industry had boomed during the war, helped to shape the postwar world economy. The United States also led the charge to establish the United Nations (UN). While it was organized on the basis of the Great Powers, all member nations sat on the General Assembly. In 1948, the UN issued the Universal Declaration of Human Rights, which condemns slavery and torture, upholds freedom of speech and religion, and affirms the right to an adequate standard of living.

During the war, the Axis Powers had repeatedly violated the Geneva Convention, which governs the humane treatment of wounded soldiers and prisoners of war. More than a thousand Japanese were tried for war crimes, and at the Nuremberg Trials, key leaders of Nazi Germany were brought to justice for their crimes against humanity.

Americans had closely followed the war and learned to think in global terms. They defined themselves as democratic, tolerant, and peaceful. The war gave renewed vigor to the fight for civil rights at home. It also ushered in a period of economic growth and prosperity.

Lesson Vocabulary

superpowers strong nations that dominated the postwar world

Copyright © by Pearson Education, Inc., or its affiliates. All Rights Reserved.

Name _____ Class _____ Date _____

TOPIC 14: Review Questions
WORLD WAR II

Answer the questions below using the information in the Lesson Summaries on the previous pages.

Lesson 1: Rise of Aggressive Dictators

1. **Summarize** Name the countries and leaders discussed in this section.
_____
_____

2. How did the military leaders of Japan want to solve the country's problems?
_____
_____

Lesson 2: America Debates Involvement

3. What was President Roosevelt's position on the war in Europe?
_____
_____

4. **Sequence** List the countries Germany conquered by order of date.
_____
_____

Lesson 3: America Enters World War II

5. **Identify Causes and Effects** What was the United States' immediate reaction to the attack on Pearl Harbor?
_____
_____

6. Why was the Battle of Coral Sea so important to the United States?
_____
_____

Lesson 4: A War on Two Fronts

7. Why was it so important for the United States to defeat the Japanese at Midway?
_____
_____

8. **Summarize** How did the Allies prepare for the invasion of Italy?
_____
_____

Name _____ Class _____ Date _____

Topic 14 Review Questions
WORLD WAR II (continued)

Lesson 5: The Home Front
9. What was the bracero program?
_____
_____

10. **Identify Main Ideas** How did the workplace change as a result of World War II?
_____
_____

Lesson 6: The Allies Win World War II
11. What was involved in the D-Day invasion of France?
_____
_____

12. **Recognize Sequence** Number the following events in chronological order.

　Japan surrenders.

　The first atomic bomb is tested.

　Germany surrenders.
_____
_____

Lesson 7: The Holocaust
13. What was the purpose of Hitler's concentration camps?
_____
_____

14. **Recognize Sequence** What happened to Jews in Germany after Hitler came to power?
_____
_____

Lesson 8: Impact of World War II
15. What long-term changes were brought about by World War II?
_____
_____

16. **Understand Effects** Which effect of World War II would help to prevent future wars?
_____
_____

Copyright © by Pearson Education, Inc., or its affiliates. All Rights Reserved.

Name _____ Class _____ Date _____

TOPIC 15
Note Taking Study Guide
POSTWAR AMERICA

Focus Question: How did the United States and its Allies resist the spread of communism throughout the world? How was this done both politically and socially?

As you read, note specific examples of how the United States resisted communism through international actions as well as through domestic changes.

Resistance to Communism	
International Actions	**Domestic Changes**
1.	1.
2.	2.
3.	3.
4.	4.
5.	5.
6.	6.
7.	7.
8.	8.

TOPIC 15 LESSON 1

Lesson Summary
THE BEGINNING OF THE COLD WAR

MODIFIED CORNELL NOTES

When Roosevelt, Stalin, and Churchill met at Yalta in February 1945, it was clear that the Allies would defeat Germany. The United States and Great Britain wanted a united Germany and independent nations in Eastern Europe after the war. Soviet dictator Stalin wanted a weak, divided Germany and an Eastern Europe under communist control. Despite Stalin's promises, Poland, Czechoslovakia, Hungary, Romania, and Bulgaria became **satellite states** of the Soviet Union, along with the eastern part of Germany. After another meeting that summer at Potsdam, Harry S. Truman, who was now President, became convinced that the Soviet Union had aspirations toward world domination. Thus began the 46-year long Cold War.

Churchill agreed with President Truman and said an **iron curtain** had descended upon Europe. East of the curtain, Stalin was tightening his grip and trying to spread communism to other countries. Truman asked Congress for money to help Turkey and Greece fight communism. His promise of aid became known as the Truman Doctrine. It set a new course for American foreign policy.

The goal of another American policy, called **containment**, was to use American power to help nations resist communism. Containment's first success was based on Secretary of State George C. Marshall's economic recovery plan for Europe. Under the Marshall Plan, which began in 1948, the United States gave about $13 billion in grants and loans to Western European nations.

In June 1948, Stalin decided to block all shipping from western Germany into West Berlin—deep inside communist East Germany—hoping that would make the city fall to the communists. The United States and Britain stopped his plan by airlifting supplies, including food, fuel, and clothing, into West Berlin.

The Berlin Airlift showed that communism could be contained. To continue to block Soviet expansion, the North Atlantic Treaty Organization (NATO), formed in 1949. Twelve Western European and North American nations agreed to act together to defend Western Europe. In 1955, West Germany joined NATO. In response, the Soviet Union and its satellite states formed the Warsaw Pact. All communist states of Eastern Europe except Yugoslavia promised to defend one another if attacked.

Lesson Vocabulary

satellite states independent nations under the control of a more powerful nation

iron curtain term coined by Winston Churchill to describe the border between the Soviet satellite states and Western Europe

containment policy of keeping communism contained within its existing borders

Name _____ Class _____ Date _____

TOPIC 15 LESSON 2
Lesson Summary
THE KOREAN WAR

MODIFIED CORNELL NOTES

Since the Russian Revolution, the Soviets had tried to export communism around the world, sure that it would reach worldwide influence. Events in China in 1949 seemed to prove them right.

Chinese nationalist leader Jiang Jieshi (known as Chiang Kaishek in the United States) and communist leader Mao Zedong had been allies against Japan during World War II, but once the war ended, they became enemies. The United States supported Jiang, while the Soviet Union aided Mao. In 1949, Mao's communists took over the Chinese mainland, calling their government the People's Republic of China.

From there, the conflict over communism moved to Korea. After World War II, the United States and the Soviet Union had split Korea into two nations divided by the 38th parallel of latitude. On June 25, 1950, about 90,000 North Korean troops armed with Soviet weapons crossed the 38th parallel to attack South Korea.

President Truman sent American troops to join South Korean and United Nations forces. Under a World War II hero, General Douglas MacArthur, they attacked the port city of Inchon in September 1950. By October, they drove the North Koreans back north.

Truman worried what China might do if the war continued, but MacArthur told him China would not intervene and he continued to push northward. Then, on November 26, 1950, around 300,000 Chinese soldiers attacked. Truman did not want the United States to enter into a major war that would involve huge numbers of troops and maybe even atomic weapons, but MacArthur distrusted Truman's policy of a "**limited war**." When MacArthur sent a letter to Congress condemning the policy, Truman fired him.

By the spring of 1951, the war settled into a stalemate. To achieve a cease-fire in 1953, Dwight D. Eisenhower, now President, hinted he might use nuclear weapons.

No side won the Korean War, and the two Koreas remain divided today. But two things did change: Truman's use of American forces enlarged the power of the presidency, and a new alliance called the Southeast Asia Treaty Organization (SEATO) was formed to prevent the spread of communism. It was the Asian version of NATO.

Lesson Vocabulary

limited war   worldwide rivalry between the United States and the Soviet Union

Name _____ Class _____ Date _____

Topic 15 Lesson 3
Lesson Summary
THE COLD WAR INTENSIFIES

MODIFIED CORNELL NOTES

On September 2, 1949, Americans learned that the Soviets now had an atomic bomb. The following month, communists took over China. For Americans, the world had suddenly become more threatening.

Truman soon ordered the development of a hydrogen bomb. Some scientists warned that developing the H-Bomb would lead to a perpetual **arms race**. For the next four decades, the United States and the Soviet Union stockpiled nuclear weapons. Each hoped this program of **mutually assured destruction** would prevent the other from actually using the weapons.

President Dwight D. Eisenhower continued to stockpile nuclear weapons. His foreign policy emphasized **massive retaliation**. Eisenhower's Secretary of State, John Foster Dulles, believed that only by going to the brink of war—an approach called **brinksmanship**—could the United States discourage communist aggression.

Nikita Khrushchev, who became leader of the Soviet Union in 1953, continued to try to spread communism. In 1956, workers in Poland rioted against Soviet rule and won greater control of their government. But when students and workers in Hungary tried a similar thing, Khrushchev crushed the revolt.

In the Middle East, Egyptian President Gamal Abdel Nasser wanted to build a dam on the Nile River. When he opened relations with communist China and the Soviet Union, the United States withdrew its offer to help. Nasser then **nationalized** the Suez Canal. In response, Britain, France, and Israel invaded Egypt in October 1956. Using the Suez crisis as an excuse, Britain and France took control of the canal but withdrew when Eisenhower would not support them.

Eisenhower then announced the United States would use force to help any nation threatened by communism. The Eisenhower Doctrine was used in 1958 to put down a revolt against a pro-American government in Lebanon. The Eisenhower administration also used the Central Intelligence Agency (CIA) to help return pro-American governments to Iran and Guatemala.

Lesson Vocabulary

arms race competition between superpowers to build more powerful nuclear weapons

mutually assured destruction policy in which the United States and the Soviet Union hoped to deter nuclear war by building up enough weapons to destroy one another

massive retaliation policy of threatening to use massive force in response to aggression

brinksmanship belief that only by going to the brink of war could the United States protect itself against Soviet aggression

nationalized to place a private resource under government control

Name _____ Class _____ Date _____

TOPIC 15 LESSON 4

Lesson Summary
COLD WAR FEARS AT HOME

MODIFIED CORNELL NOTES

In 1947, the Red Scare—public fear that communists were working to destroy America both from within and without the country—spurred President Truman to investigate federal employees. About 3,000 people were dismissed or resigned. The Truman administration also used the 1940 Smith Act, a law against advocating violent overthrow of the government, to send 11 U.S. Communist Party members to prison.

Meanwhile, the House Committee on Un-American Activities (HUAC) investigated **subversive** activities throughout American life, including academic institutions, labor unions, and city halls. In 1947, HUAC targeted the Hollywood Ten, a group of left-wing writers, directors, and producers. They refused to testify against themselves but were sent to prison. Movie executives then circulated a **blacklist** that named entertainment figures suspected of communist ties, shattering many careers.

Two sensational spy trials increased the country's suspicion of communists. The first one concerned Alger Hiss, a government employee who had helped organize the United Nations. In 1948, Whittaker Chambers, a former member of the Communist Party and an espionage agent, named Hiss as one of his government contacts. Hiss denied everything before HUAC but was sentenced to five years in prison. The second trial involved Julius and Ethel Rosenberg, who were accused of passing secret information about nuclear science to Soviet agents. The Rosenbergs claimed that they were being persecuted because they were Jewish and held unpopular beliefs. They were convicted in a highly controversial trial and executed in 1953.

Joseph R. McCarthy, a senator from Wisconsin, also increased Americans' fears. He claimed he had a long list of communists in the State Department, but each time he was asked to give specific names and numbers, his figures changed. Still, with the outbreak of the Korean War in 1950, McCarthy's popularity soared. McCarthyism became a catchword for the senator's vicious style of reckless charges. McCarthy's targets grew bigger, and in 1954, he went after the United States Army. After viewers saw him badger witnesses and twist the truth during televised hearings, he lost his strongest supporters. The end of the Korean War in 1953 and McCarthy's downfall in 1954 signaled the decline of the Red Scare.

Lesson Vocabulary

subversive   describing a secretive act done with the intention of overthrowing or destroying a government or political system

blacklist   list of persons who were not hired because of suspected communist ties

TOPIC 15, LESSON 5

Lesson Summary
POSTWAR PROSPERITY

MODIFIED CORNELL NOTES

The production of military supplies halted at the end of World War II. Millions of Americans initially lost their jobs, but soon the nation experienced the longest period of economic growth in American history.

President Harry Truman brought soldiers home by starting the **demobilization**, or the process of sending home members of the army. To calm fears about the economy, the government passed the law known as the GI Bill of Rights. The GI Bill provided veterans with unemployment benefits, financial aid for college, and loans to start businesses.

Many veterans started families upon returning home. This **baby boom** peaked in 1957 when 4.3 million babies were born. Between 1940 and 1955, the U.S. population grew by 27 percent. Soaring demand for consumer products caused skyrocketing prices and inflation.

Southern and western states, known as the Sunbelt, also experienced rapid growth. These states had appealing climates and a large number of jobs in the defense, aerospace, and electronics industries. As people moved, their political power moved with them. The Sunbelt and suburbs gained representation while urban areas in the Northeast and the Midwest lost political power.

The U.S. economy was also shifting. Fewer people worked in manufacturing or farming. Employment grew in the **service sector**, businesses that provided services rather than manufactured goods, and **information industries**, businesses that provided informational services. **Franchise businesses** allowed companies to distribute their products and services through retail outlets owned by independent operators. **Multinational corporations**, companies that produced and sold their goods and services across the globe, thrived.

(Continues on the next page.)

Lesson Vocabulary

demobilization   sending home members of the army

baby boom   increase in births between 1945 and 1964

service sector   businesses that provide services rather than manufactured goods

information industries   businesses that provide informational services

franchise businesses   to allow companies to distribute their products or services through retail outlets owned by independent operators

multinational corporations   companies that produce and sell their goods and services all over the world

Name _____ Class _____ Date _____

TOPIC 15 LESSON 5

Lesson Summary
POSTWAR PROSPERITY (continued)

MODIFIED CORNELL NOTES

Unions also experienced change. The AFL and the CIO joined in 1955 to form the AFL-CIO, bringing them more political clout. However, new white-collar workers generally did not join unions.

The inflation rate prompted several trade unions to demand pay increases. When employers refused, millions of workers went on strike. Congress then enacted the Taft-Hartley Act to outlaw the closed shop—a workplace that hired only union members.

After the election, Truman introduced the Fair Deal, a program that would strengthen New Deal reforms and establish programs such as national health insurance. Most of the Fair Deal failed in Congress.

In 1952, Republican Dwight Eisenhower won the presidency by a landslide. He helped create an interstate highway system and gave financial support to education.

Name _____ Class _____ Date _____

TOPIC 15 LESSON 6
Lesson Summary
MASS CULTURE IN THE 1950s

MODIFIED CORNELL NOTES

Between 1940 and 1960, more than 40 million Americans moved to the suburbs, one of the largest mass migrations in history. Developers quickly began building affordable housing in the suburbs to fill the gap left by a shortage of urban housing. Government-backed low-interest loans enabled more people to purchase homes.

Suburban growth would not have been possible had Congress not passed the Interstate Highway Act in 1956. This act authorized funds to build 41,000 miles of highway, consisting of multilane expressways that would connect the nation's major cities. The new highways eased the commute from suburbs to cities and boosted the travel and vacation industries.

As the U.S. economy began to boom in the postwar era, Americans were caught up in a wave of **consumerism**, buying as much as they could, much of it on credit. **Median family income** refers to average family income. Median family income rose dramatically during the 1950s. With money to spend, easy credit, and new goods to buy, shopping became a new pastime for Americans.

During the 1950s, the ideal family was one in which men worked and women stayed home. Popular magazines of the era described the **nuclear family**, or a household consisting of a mother and father and their children, as the backbone of American society. Nevertheless, as the 1950s progressed, more women were willing to challenge the view that a woman should not have a career.

More so than in the past, family life revolved around children. Dr. Benjamin Spock, a best-selling author of the era, emphasized the importance of nurturing children, from their earliest days as infants through their teen years.

Television had a profound impact on American society, particularly among children. Sitcoms, which rarely discussed real-life problems, were popular. These shows reflected and reinforced the ideal of the 1950s family. Television also eroded distinct regional and ethnic cultures, helping to develop a national culture.

Educational opportunities grew as well. By the early 1960s, almost 40 percent of college-age Americans attended college, up from about 15 percent in 1940. The federal government increased education funds, in part to produce more scientists and science teachers. Many states improved their public universities. Ordinary Americans' access to higher education also increased. California created a California Master Plan, creating three tiers of higher education: research universities, state colleges, and community colleges.

Lesson Vocabulary

consumerism large-scale buying, much of it on credit
median family income a measure of average family income
nuclear family an ideal or typical household with a father, mother, and children

Name _____ Class _____ Date _____

TOPIC 15 LESSON 7

Lesson Summary
SOCIAL ISSUES OF THE 1950s

MODIFIED CORNELL NOTES

Despite the prosperity of the 1950s, not everyone benefited from it. Some Americans were dissatisfied with the changes brought by affluence. Social critics and a small group of writers and artists known as **beatniks** criticized what they viewed as the crass materialism and conformity of the American middle class. The theme of alienation, or the feeling of being cut off from mainstream society, dominated many of the era's popular novels.

Like television, **rock-and-roll** captured the attention of Americans. Rock music originated in the rhythm and blues traditions of African Americans. Elvis Presley made rock music popular when he integrated African American gospel tunes into the music he played. Although some Americans complained about rock music, it nonetheless became a symbol of the emerging youth culture and of the growing power of youth on mass culture.

Hidden behind this prosperity were urban slums, desperate rural poverty, and discrimination. Michael Harrington's influential book *The Other America* (1962) opened Americans' eyes to the 50 million people, one fourth of the nation, living in poverty. Many of the "invisible" poor were inner-city African Americans, rural whites, and Latinos in migrant farm camps and urban barrios.

As the middle class moved from cities to the suburbs, cities lost revenue and political clout. Minorities moved in great numbers to cities in search of better economic opportunities. Strained city services, such as garbage removal, deteriorated. Crime increased in what was now called the inner city, further encouraging middle-class Americans to flee. Government-funded **urban renewal** projects tried to reverse this trend by creating developments that they hoped would revitalize downtowns. Many failed, pushing people from their homes into already overcrowded areas.

(Continues on the next page.)

Lesson Vocabulary

beatniks small group of writers and artists, in the 1950s and early 1960s, who were critical of American society

rock-and-roll popular music that grew out of the gospel and blues traditions of African Americans

urban renewal government programs for redevelopment of urban areas

Name _____ Class _____ Date _____

TOPIC 15
LESSON 7

Lesson Summary
SOCIAL ISSUES OF THE 1950s (continued)

MODIFIED CORNELL NOTES

Many of the rural poor also relocated to cities. Small farmers slipped into poverty when they could not compete with corporations and large-farm owners dominating agricultural production.

Efforts to overcome housing and employment discrimination became central to the struggle for civil rights. Latinos and Native Americans struggled with many of the same problems. In 1953, the federal government enacted the **termination policy**, a law that sought to end tribal government and to relocate Native Americans to the nation's cities. Proponents of the policy argued that it would better enable American Indians to assimilate into American society.

Lesson Vocabulary

termination policy   a policy ending all programs monitored by the Bureau of Indian Affairs. It also ended federal responsibility for the health and welfare of Native Americans.

Name _____ Class _____ Date _____

TOPIC 15 — Review Questions
POSTWAR AMERICA

Answer the questions below using the information in the Lesson Summaries on the previous pages.

Lesson 1: The Beginning of the Cold War

1. Which event proved that the policy of containment worked?
   _____
   _____

2. **Contrast** After World War II, what were the differences in goals between Stalin and the Soviets and Truman and the United States?
   _____
   _____

Lesson 2: The Korean War

3. **Categorize** What idea and event led directly to Truman's firing of MacArthur?
   _____
   _____

4. What is the significance of the 38th parallel?
   _____
   _____

Lesson 3: The Cold War Intensifies

5. **Identify Main Ideas** Describe the ways the United States and the Soviet Union competed with each other for supremacy.
   _____
   _____

6. How were brinksmanship and massive retaliation supposed to deter communist aggression?
   _____
   _____

Lesson 4: Cold War Fears at Home

7. How were the Smith Act and HUAC supposed to discourage communism in the United States?
   _____
   _____

8. **Identify Causes and Effects** Discuss the events that led to McCarthyism and the popularity of the senator from Wisconsin.
   _____
   _____

Name _____ Class _____ Date _____

TOPIC 15 Review Questions
POSTWAR AMERICA (continued)

Lesson 5: Postwar Prosperity

9. What is the Taft-Hartley Act? Why was it passed?

10. **Understand Effects** How did the GI Bill benefit the American economy?

Lesson 6: Mass Culture in the 1950s

11. Discuss the factors that fostered suburban growth.

12. **Identify Main Ideas** Discuss changes in American education in the postwar period.

Lesson 7 Social Issues of the 1950s

13. **Identify Main Ideas** How did television and rock-and-roll impact postwar American society?

14. Discuss how cities changed during this period.

Name _____ Class _____ Date _____

TOPIC 16
Note Taking Study Guide
CIVIL RIGHTS AND REFORM IN THE 1960s

Focus Question: In what ways did significant social change come to America in the 1960s?

As you read, note specific examples that support the idea that American society changed significantly during the 1960s.

Social Change in the '60s

Name _____ Class _____ Date _____

TOPIC 16 LESSON 1
Lesson Summary
THE CIVIL RIGHTS MOVEMENT STRENGTHENS

MODIFIED CORNELL NOTES

After World War II, Jim Crow laws in the South continued to enforce strict separation of the races. Segregation that is imposed by law is known as **de jure segregation**. African Americans also faced segregation in the North, even where there were no explicit laws. **De facto segregation**, or segregation by unwritten custom, was a fact of life.

Thurgood Marshall, an African American lawyer, worked with civil rights organizations to challenge segregation in the courts. In 1954, *Brown* v. *Board of Education* challenged segregated public education at all grade levels. Chief Justice Earl Warren wrote the *Brown* decision in which the Supreme Court agreed that segregated public schools violated the United States Constitution. The *Brown* decision overturned the principle of "separate but equal." It also lent support to the view that all forms of segregation were wrong.

In Little Rock, Arkansas, the governor ordered the National Guard to block nine African American students from entering a high school. President Eisenhower sent federal troops to protect the students and to enforce the Court's decision. However, southern states continued to resist compliance with the law.

Congress passed the Civil Rights Act of 1957. This act established the U.S. Civil Rights Commission. The law's main significance was that it was the first civil rights bill passed by Congress since Reconstruction. It was a small, but important, victory.

In 1955, an African American woman named Rosa Parks refused to give up her bus seat to a white passenger in Montgomery, Alabama. She was arrested. A core of civil rights activists in Montgomery organized a one-day bus boycott to express opposition to Park's arrest and to segregation in general.

The next evening, Dr. Martin Luther King, Jr., a Baptist minister, gave an inspirational speech in which he called upon African Americans to protest segregation and oppression in a nonviolent manner. The Montgomery bus boycott continued for more than a year. In 1956, the Supreme Court ruled that the Montgomery city law that segregated buses was unconstitutional. The boycott revealed the power African Americans could have if they joined together. It also helped King and his philosophy of nonviolence to gain prominence within the civil rights movement.

Lesson Vocabulary

de jure segregation   segregation imposed by law

de facto segregation   segregation by unwritten custom or tradition

Name _____ Class _____ Date _____

MODIFIED CORNELL NOTES

TOPIC 16 LESSON 2

Lesson Summary
THE MOVEMENT SURGES FORWARD

Despite some victories, activists continued to struggle for African Americans' civil rights. In North Carolina, four college students started a sit-in to protest discrimination. This **sit-in** sparked a wave of similar protests across the nation. Young African American activists established the Student Nonviolent Coordinating Committee (SNCC), to create a grass-roots movement to gain equality.

The next battleground was interstate transportation. The Supreme Court had ruled that segregation on interstate buses was illegal. In the spring of 1961, the Congress of Racial Equality (CORE) stage a **freedom ride** through the Deep South to test the federal government's willingness to enforce the law. After the freedom riders were met with violence, President John F. Kennedy intervened. Mississippi's leaders agreed to send police to protect the riders.

In September 1962, James Meredith won a federal court case that allowed him to enroll at the all-white University of Mississippi. Civil rights activist Medgar Evers was instrumental in this effort. Although full-scale riots erupted the night before his arrival, Meredith went on to graduate from the university in 1963.

In the spring of 1963, Martin Luther King, Jr., and the Southern Christian Leadership Conference (SCLC) targeted Birmingham, Alabama, for a major civil rights campaign. The campaign began nonviolently with protest marches and sit-ins. However, Birmingham's Public Safety Commissioner refused to tolerate the demonstrations. He used police dogs and fire hoses on the peaceful protesters. News coverage of the violence shocked many Americans.

To put pressure on Congress to pass a new civil rights bill, supporters organized a massive demonstration in Washington, D.C. More than 200,000 Americans gathered for the March on Washington on August 28, 1963. The highlight of the day came when King gave his "I Have a Dream" speech.

On November 22, 1963, President Kennedy was assassinated. Vice President Lyndon B. Johnson assumed the presidency. Johnson used his political skills to gain the passage of the Civil Rights Act of 1964, which banned segregation in public accommodations. The surge in support for the civil rights movement had produced a dramatic shift in race relations and set the stage for future reforms.

Lesson Vocabulary

sit-in form of protest during which participants sit and refuse to move

freedom ride 1961 protest by activists who rode buses through southern states to test their compliance with laws banning segregation on interstate buses

Copyright © by Pearson Education, Inc., or its affiliates. All Rights Reserved.

Name _____ Class _____ Date _____

TOPIC 16 LESSON 3
Lesson Summary
SUCCESSES AND SETBACKS

MODIFIED CORNELL NOTES

Although the civil rights movement had made progress, the southern political system still prevented African Americans from voting. In 1964, the SNCC mounted a major voter registration project, known as Freedom Summer. About 1,000 volunteers flooded Mississippi to register African Americans to vote.

In Selma, Alabama, Martin Luther King, Jr., and the SCLC organized a campaign to pressure the government to enact voting rights legislation. The protests climaxed in a series of confrontations, as heavily armed state troopers attacked the marchers. Spurred by the actions of the protesters, Congress passed the Voting Rights Act of 1965, which banned literacy tests. Another legal landmark was the Twenty-fourth Amendment, ratified in 1964. This amendment banned the poll tax, which had been used to prevent poor African Americans from voting.

Still, for some African Americans, things had not changed much. In many urban areas, anger over continuing discrimination and poverty erupted into violence and race riots. To determine the causes of the riots, President Johnson established the Kerner Commission. The commission concluded that long-term racial discrimination was the single most important cause of violence.

The riots coincided with the radicalization of many young urban African Americans. Malcolm X was the most well-known African American radical. Malcolm X became a prominent minister of the Nation of Islam, a religious sect that demanded separation of the races. However, he was assassinated in February 1965.

Many young African Americans considered themselves heirs of Malcolm X and moved away from the principle of nonviolence. SNCC leader Stokely Carmichael thought that African Americans should use their economic and political muscle, which he termed **"black power,"** to gain equality. Not long after, militants formed the Black Panther Party. Almost overnight, the Black Panthers became the symbol of young militant African Americans.

On April 4, 1968, Martin Luther King, Jr., was assassinated. In the wake of his murder, Congress passed the Fair Housing Act, which banned discrimination in housing. Although African Americans had made significant gains, the radicalism of the times left a bitter legacy.

Lesson Vocabulary

"black power" economic and political muscle of African Americans

Copyright © by Pearson Education, Inc., or its affiliates. All Rights Reserved.

Name _____ Class _____ Date _____

TOPIC 16 LESSON 4 — Lesson Summary
KENNEDY'S REFORMS

MODIFIED CORNELL NOTES

The 1960 election featured Democrat John F. Kennedy and Republican Richard M. Nixon. Both were young, energetic, and intelligent. Kennedy won the election narrowly, in part due to an impressive performance in a televised debate.

President Kennedy promised Americans that his administration would blaze a "New Frontier." The term described Kennedy's proposals to improve the economy, education, healthcare, and civil rights. He used his charisma and a team of intelligent advisers to win support for his programs.

The high levels of poverty in America troubled Kennedy. Congress was hesitant to make reforms, but Kennedy did achieve an increase in the minimum wage and improvements in the welfare system. He also tried to make sure that women were paid equal wages for "equal work." The Equal Pay Act required this. Although it contained various loopholes, the law was an important step on the road to fair and equal employment practices.

The economy was weak when Kennedy took office, and he thought that improving the economy would reduce poverty. Kennedy accepted the "new economics" of John Maynard Keynes that advocated **deficit spending** to stimulate the economy. Deficit spending is the government practice of borrowing money in order to spend more than is received from taxes.

At first, Kennedy moved slowly on civil rights, worried that he would lose the support of the conservatives in his party. By 1963, however, Kennedy realized that African Americans needed the federal government to protect their rights. He introduced a bill that used federal money to aid school desegregation and demanded other reforms.

Perhaps the most visual component of the New Frontier was the active space program. Americans were afraid of falling behind the Soviets in the "**space race**." Kennedy called for a man to be landed on the moon in less than 10 years. That goal was met in 1969.

Kennedy's term as President was ended by his assassination. Lee Harvey Oswald shot Kennedy while he was riding in a car in Dallas, Texas. Although many people questioned whether Oswald acted alone, the Warren Commission, which conducted the official investigation of the shooting, declared that Oswald acted alone. The senseless murder deeply saddened Americans across the nation. It seemed as if part of America's innocence had died with Kennedy.

Lesson Vocabulary

deficit spending   practice of a nation paying out more money than it is receiving in revenues

"space race"   competition between the United States and the Soviet Union to successfully land on the moon

Name _____ Class _____ Date _____

TOPIC 16 LESSON 5
Lesson Summary
REFORM UNDER JOHNSON

MODIFIED CORNELL NOTES

Lyndon B. Johnson, who became President after Kennedy's assassination, shared the same goals as his predecessor. Johnson's rise to the top was not easy. He was born in a small town in Texas. After attending a state college, he taught in a poor, segregated school for Mexican Americans. After teaching for several years, he was elected to Congress and began working his way up.

Johnson proved to be an excellent politician. One of his first successes after becoming President was ensuring that Congress passed the Civil Rights Act, an important bill introduced by President Kennedy. This bill was a major victory in the struggle to end discrimination in voting, education, and **public accommodations**.

The War on Poverty was a big part of Johnson's plans. He wanted to provide more training, education, and healthcare to those who needed it. The Economic Opportunity Act began this process by creating agencies such as Job Corps, VISTA, and Head Start.

After being elected President in 1964, Johnson called his vision for America the Great Society. He said the Great Society demanded "an end to poverty and racial injustice." In 1965, Congress began to pass Johnson's Great Society legislation.

One area of reform was in healthcare insurance. Johnson created Medicare, a program that provided basic hospital insurance for older Americans. He also created Medicaid, which provided basic medical services to poor and disabled Americans.

Education and immigration policy also saw reforms. The 1965 Elementary and Secondary Education Act aided schools in poorer communities. The Immigration and Nationality Act of 1965 relaxed the nation's immigration policies. Over the next two decades, millions of immigrants poured into the United States.

During the 1960s, the Supreme Court was also interested in reform. The court decided cases on controversial social, religious, and political issues. Led by Chief Justice Earl Warren—and often called the Warren Court—this liberal court supported civil rights, **civil liberties**, voting rights, and personal privacy.

Lesson Vocabulary

public accommodations   public or private establishments, such as schools, that are used by the public

civil liberties   freedom of the people from unwarranted government interference as guaranteed by the Bill of Rights

Name _____ Class _____ Date _____

TOPIC 16 Review Questions
CIVIL RIGHTS AND REFORM IN THE 1960s

Answer the questions below using the information in the Lesson Summaries on the previous pages.

Lesson 1: The Civil Rights Movement Strengthens

1. Explain the importance of *Brown* v. *Board of Education*.
_____
_____

2. Summarize List three key events of the 1950s that helped to end segregation.
_____
_____

Lesson 2: The Movement Surges Forward

3. What was the purpose of the March on Washington?
_____
_____

4. Summarize Summarize the significance of James Meredith's actions in 1962.
_____
_____

Lesson 3 Successes and Setbacks

5. Explain the significance of the march in Selma
_____
_____

6. Summarize Summarize the impact of Malcolm X on the civil rights movement.
_____
_____

Lesson 4: Kennedy's Reforms

7. What did Kennedy do to advance the space program?
_____
_____

8. Identify Main Ideas What was deficit spending and why did Kennedy support it?
_____
_____

Copyright © by Pearson Education, Inc., or its affiliates. All Rights Reserved.

Name _____ Class _____ Date _____

TOPIC 16 Review Questions
CIVIL RIGHTS AND REFORM IN THE 1960s (continued)

Lesson 5: Reform Under Johnson

9. **Identify Main Ideas** What did the Civil Rights Act accomplish?
_____
_____

10. What programs did Johnson create to fight poverty?
_____
_____

Name _____ Class _____ Date _____

TOPIC 17
Note Taking Study Guide
THE VIETNAM WAR ERA

Focus Question: Why were some people in favor of U.S. military involvement in Vietnam and other people against it?

As you read, take notes in the following chart to summarize the content of this topic. Note specific examples of reasons why people supported and opposed U.S. military involvement in Vietnam.

Supported	Opposed
•	•
•	•
	•

Name _____ Class _____ Date _____

TOPIC 17 LESSON 1
Lesson Summary
THE COLD WAR AND VIETNAM

MODIFIED CORNELL NOTES

President Kennedy worked to build up the country's armed forces. He wanted a **flexible response** defense policy to prepare the United States to fight any size or any type of conflict. He also wanted to prevent the spread of communism in poor nations around the globe.

Kennedy's first major challenge came in Cuba. The revolutionary Fidel Castro took over Cuba in 1959 and aligned Cuba with the Soviet Union. Eisenhower had planned an invasion of Cuba to overthrow Castro, and Kennedy executed this plan in 1961. A CIA-led force of Cuban exiles attacked Cuba in the Bay of Pigs invasion. The invasion failed and probably ended up strengthening Castro's position in Cuba.

When the Soviets began building nuclear missile sites in Cuba in range of East Coast cities, Kennedy faced his third challenge. During the Cuban missile crisis, Kennedy demanded that the Soviets remove the missiles. Nuclear war seemed possible. After several tense days, Khrushchev agreed to remove the missiles. The leaders agreed to install a **hot line** telephone system between Moscow and Washington, D.C., to improve communication. A year later, in 1963, the United States, Great Britain, and the Soviet Union signed the first nuclear-weapons agreement.

Kennedy's next challenge involved the Soviet premier Nikita Khrushchev, who demanded that America remove its troops from West Berlin and recognize the divided city. Kennedy refused. Khrushchev then ordered the construction of a wall between East and West Berlin. The Berlin Wall became a symbol of the divide between communism and democracy.

France had controlled Vietnam as a colony since the 1800s. After World War II, however, a strong independence movement took hold. The movement was led by Ho Chi Minh, who had been fighting for Vietnamese independence for 30 years. Ho Chi Minh had fled Vietnam in 1912. During his travels around the world, he embraced communism and had formed ties with the Soviet Union.

(Continues on the next page.)

Lesson Vocabulary

flexible response   defense policy allowing for the appropriate action in any type of conflict

hot line   direct telephone line between the White House and the Kremlin set up after the Cuban Missile Crisis

Name _____ Class _____ Date _____

TOPIC 17 LESSON 1

Lesson Summary
THE COLD WAR AND VIETNAM (continued)

MODIFIED CORNELL NOTES

The United States became involved in Vietnam for several reasons. First, it wanted to keep France as an ally. To ensure French support in the Cold War, President Truman agreed to help France regain control over Vietnam. Second, both Truman and Eisenhower wanted to contain the spread of communism. They believed in the **domino theory**. This idea held that if Vietnam fell to communism, its closest neighbors would follow. Communism would then spread throughout the entire region.

The United States channeled aid to South Vietnam through the Southeast Asia Treaty Organization (SEATO).

In 1961, President Kennedy began sending U.S. troops to South Vietnam. President Johnson increased U.S. involvement after North Vietnam attacked a U.S. destroyer patrolling the Gulf of Tonkin. Congress passed the Gulf of Tonkin Resolution, which gave Johnson authority to use force to defend American troops. This resolution gave the President the power to commit U.S. troops to fight without asking Congress for a formal declaration of war.

Lesson Vocabulary

domino theory   idea that if a nation falls to communism, its closest neighbors will also fall under communist control

Name _____ Class _____ Date _____

TOPIC 17 LESSON 2
Lesson Summary
AMERICA'S ROLE ESCALATES

MODIFIED CORNELL NOTES

In February 1965, President Johnson took the United States deeper into the Vietnam War by ordering a large bombing campaign called Operation Rolling Thunder. Despite massive and sustained airstrikes, communist forces continued to fight. Johnson then ordered more troops to fight them on the ground. This more active strategy came primarily from Secretary of Defense Robert McNamara and General William Westmoreland, the American commander in South Vietnam.

In addition to conventional bombs, American pilots dropped napalm and sprayed Agent Orange. **Napalm** is a jellied gasoline that covered large areas in flames. Agent Orange is an herbicide that destroys plant life. It was used to disrupt the enemy's food supply.

When the U.S. troops fought on the ground, it was rarely in large battles. The Vietcong and North Vietnamese Army fought with guerilla tactics in the jungle, trying to wear the United States down because they knew they could not win a traditional war. They followed Ho Chi Minh's doctrine, which stated that fighting should never be on the opponent's terms. Communist forces used hit-and-run attacks, nighttime ambushes, and booby traps. It was also difficult for the U.S. troops to know which Vietnamese person was a friend or an enemy.

By 1967, the war had become a stalemate. By 1968, more than 30,000 Americans had been killed in Vietnam. Despite the many times Johnson asserted that victory was near, each year yielded little progress. Troop morale began to fall.

The costs of the war had also grown each year, straining government finances. Government spending had lowered the unemployment rate at home, but it had also led to rising prices and inflation. President Johnson was forced to raise taxes, and social programs at home had to be cut.

The war was being questioned in Congress. In 1967, Congress was divided into two camps: hawks and doves. **Hawks** supported the war and believed they were fighting communism. **Doves** questioned the war on moral and strategic grounds. They were not convinced that Vietnam was a vital Cold War battleground.

Lesson Vocabulary

napalm jellied gasoline dropped in canisters that explode on impact and cover large areas in flame; dropped by U.S. planes during the Vietnam War

hawk person who supported U.S. involvement in the Vietnam War

dove person who opposed U.S. involvement in the Vietnam War

Name _____ Class _____ Date _____

Topic 17 Lesson 3: Lesson Summary
THE ANTIWAR MOVEMENT

MODIFIED CORNELL NOTES

The war in Vietnam divided Americans and opened a deep emotional rift in American society. To provide enough soldiers for the war, the government drafted young men into service. Some of these **draftees**, however, thought that the selection method was unfair. Draft boards were allowed to grant deferments to college students and men who worked in certain occupations. The result was that most of the men who served in Vietnam came from working-class and poor backgrounds. The number of African Americans in Vietnam was also disproportionately high.

College campuses became centers of antiwar sentiment. The Students for a Democratic Society (SDS), formed in 1960 to fight racism and poverty, became a leading antiwar group. College students and police clashed during antiwar demonstrations. Nightly television coverage of the war fueled opposition to the conflict. The differences between war accounts given by journalists and the optimistic progress reported by the government created a **credibility gap**.

Because of the government's reports on the war, the public was greatly surprised by the Tet Offensive. This major offensive by the North Vietnamese Army showed that the enemy was still strong. The United States repelled the offensive, but after these attacks, American leaders seemed less confident of a quick end to the war.

Meanwhile, the 1968 election campaign began. Senator Eugene McCarthy, the antiwar Democratic presidential candidate, made a surprisingly strong showing in an early primary election. Democratic senator Robert Kennedy also announced his candidacy for President. Soon thereafter, Johnson announced that he would not run for another term as President.

The spring and summer of 1968 saw violence at home. First, civil rights leader Martin Luther King, Jr., was assassinated. Then, Robert Kennedy was assassinated after winning the California primary. In August, major protests erupted at the Democratic National Convention in Chicago. Police clashed with antiwar protesters in the streets outside the convention center. The chaos and civil disorder helped Republican Richard Nixon win the presidency in 1968. Nixon promised to achieve "peace with honor" in Vietnam.

Lesson Vocabulary

draftees   young American men drafted into military service

credibility gap   American public's growing distrust of statements made by the government during the Vietnam War

Name _____ Class _____ Date _____

TOPIC 17 LESSON 4

Lesson Summary
THE WAR'S END AND EFFECTS

MODIFIED CORNELL NOTES

When Nixon became President, he believed that a peace deal could be negotiated with North Vietnam. However, when these negotiations stalled, Nixon gradually began to pull American troops out of Vietnam. He believed that the South Vietnamese army should fight on its own and called this approach **Vietnamization**. He hoped that sending American supplies to the South Vietnamese Army would be sufficient for the army to secure and hold South Vietnam.

In 1970, however, Nixon ordered a ground attack on communists in Cambodia, which angered antiwar activists at home. They claimed that Nixon was widening the war, not ending it. Protests erupted on many college campuses. At Kent State University, members of the National Guard fired into a crowd of protesters, killing four. This led to demonstrations on other campuses, including Jackson State in Mississippi, where two students were killed.

Other events also outraged the public. American troops killed more than 400 unarmed Vietnamese in the village of My Lai. The Pentagon Papers showed that the government had been dishonest with the public and with Congress about the Vietnam War.

American bombing finally induced the North Vietnamese to resume negotiations. In January 1973, the United States, South Vietnam, North Vietnam, and the Vietcong signed the Paris Peace Accords. American troops would withdraw from South Vietnam, and North Vietnamese troops would remain in South Vietnam. The war was over for the United States, but the fighting continued in Vietnam. The Soviet-supplied North Vietnamese Army defeated the South Vietnamese Army, and Vietnam was united under a communist regime.

More than 58,000 American troops and over 2 million Vietnamese had been killed in the Vietnam War. Turmoil troubled Southeast Asia for many years afterward. After the difficult experience in Vietnam, Americans were less willing to intervene in the affairs of other countries. Americans also had less trust in their leaders. In 1973, Congress passed the War Powers Act, which restricted the President's authority to commit American troops to foreign conflicts. The fear of "another Vietnam" would affect American foreign policy for decades to come.

Lesson Vocabulary

Vietnamization   President Nixon's plan for gradual withdrawal of U.S. forces as South Vietnamese troops assumed more combat duties

Copyright © by Pearson Education, Inc., or its affiliates. All Rights Reserved.

Name _____ Class _____ Date _____

TOPIC 17: Review Questions
THE VIETNAM WAR ERA

Answer the questions below using the information in the Lesson Summaries on the previous pages.

Lesson 1: The Cold War and Vietnam

1. **Summarize** Why did the United States help France in Vietnam?
_____
_____

2. What was the domino theory?
_____
_____

Lesson 2: America's Role Escalates

3. Which group in Congress opposed the war in Vietnam?
_____
_____

4. **Identify Supporting Details** Why did President Johnson raise taxes?
_____
_____

Lesson 3: The Antiwar Movement

5. Why did some people think that the draft system was unfair?
_____
_____

6. **Recognize Sequence** How did the protests at the Democratic National Convention in 1968 help Richard Nixon?
_____
_____

Lesson 4: The War's End and Effects

7. Why did the Pentagon Papers outrage Americans?
_____
_____

8. **Recognize Effects** What was one effect of the Vietnam War on American foreign policy?
_____
_____

Copyright © by Pearson Education, Inc., or its affiliates. All Rights Reserved.

Name _____ Class _____ Date _____

TOPIC 18
Note Taking Study Guide
AN ERA OF CHANGE

Focus Question: How did the activist movements of the 1960s and 1970s shape America?

As you read, take notes in the chart below. Note one specific example of what each of the activist movements described in this Topic achieved in the 1960s and 1970s.

Activist Movements and Achievements

Movement:	Movement:	Movement:	Movement:
Achievements:	Achievements:	Achievements:	Achievements:

Copyright © by Pearson Education, Inc., or its affiliates. All Rights Reserved.
167

Name _____ Class _____ Date _____

Topic 18 Lesson 1

Lesson Summary
THE COUNTERCULTURE OF THE 1960s

MODIFIED CORNELL NOTES

The **counterculture** grew out of the Beat movement's emphasis on freedom from materialism and the civil rights movement's questioning of traditional boundaries. The antiwar movement's distrust of authority, sparked by the Vietnam War, fostered a spirit of rebellion. Members of the counterculture, known as hippies, valued youth, spontaneity, and individuality, and promoted peace, love, and freedom. Their experimentation with drugs, new styles of dress and music, and freer attitudes toward sexual relationships contradicted traditional values and boundaries. This rebellion led to a misunderstanding between the older and younger generation, a situation that was called a **generation gap**.

Born after World War II, the younger generation had an enormous influence on American society, driving changes in attitudes and styles in everything from clothes to music and art. Rock-and-roll music by bands such as the Beatles came to define the decade. Hippies rejected many traditional restrictions on sexual behavior in what became known as the "sexual revolution." Many also often adopted new living patterns, residing in **communes**, small communities where people shared interests and resources.

The center of the counterculture was the Haight-Ashbury district of San Francisco. There, hippies experimented with drugs and listened to rock music and speeches by political radicals such as Timothy Leary, who encouraged youths to "tune in," "turn on" to drugs, and "drop out" of mainstream society.

Some hippies sought spirituality outside of the Judeo-Christian tradition, exploring Eastern religions and practices of Native Americans. Some sought to live off the land in harmony with nature. These beliefs impacted the growing environmental movement.

By the late 1960s, several key figures of the counterculture died from drug overdoses, and many people had become disillusioned with the movement's excesses. Most hippies eventually rejoined the mainstream, but the seeds of protest sown during the 1960s would influence the growing "rights revolution."

Lesson Vocabulary

counterculture movement that upheld values different from those of mainstream culture

generation gap lack of understanding and communication between older and younger members of society

communes small communities where people with common interests live and share resources

Name _____ Class _____ Date _____

TOPIC 18 LESSON 2
Lesson Summary
THE WOMEN'S RIGHTS MOVEMENT

MODIFIED CORNELL NOTES

The first wave of feminism began in the 1840s and culminated in 1920 with women winning the right to vote. **Feminism** is the theory of political, social, and economic equality for men and women. The second wave of feminism was born in the 1960s. Inspired by successes of the civil rights movement, women wanted to change how they were treated as a group and to redefine how they were viewed as individuals.

The role of housewife was seen as the proper one for women, but many women found it deeply unsatisfying. Those women who did work experienced open and routine discrimination, including being paid less than men. Betty Friedan described women's dissatisfaction in her 1963 book *The Feminine Mystique*. Friedan later helped establish the National Organization for Women (NOW), which sought to win equality for women. The group campaigned for passage of the Equal Rights Amendment (ERA), an amendment to the Constitution that would guarantee gender equality under the law. NOW also worked to protect women's right to abortions. Radical feminists went further, conducting protests to expose discrimination against women. One radical feminist was Gloria Steinem, who sought to raise consciousness through the media and helped co-found *Ms.* magazine in 1972.

Not all women supported these efforts. Phyllis Schlafly, a conservative political activist, denounced women's liberation as "a total assault on the family, on marriage, and on children." The ERA failed to pass partly due to her efforts.

Women did, however, gain new legal rights. Title IX of the Higher Education Act of 1972 banned discrimination in education and the Equal Credit Opportunity Act made it illegal to deny credit to a woman on the basis of gender. The 1973 Supreme Court decision in *Roe* v. *Wade* gave women the right to legal abortions.

Changes in the workplace came slowly. Today, more women work, and more work in fields such as medicine and law that were once restricted to them. Despite these gains, the average woman still earns less than the average man, partly because women continue to work in fields that pay less.

Lesson Vocabulary

feminism theory that women and men should have political, social, and economic equality

Copyright © by Pearson Education, Inc., or its affiliates. All Rights Reserved.

Topic 18, Lesson 3 — Lesson Summary
EXPANDING THE PUSH FOR EQUALITY

MODIFIED CORNELL NOTES

Mexican and other Latin American immigrants came to the United States during and after World War II, filling the need for cheap labor. Mexican immigrants came as temporary farmworkers. Other immigrants came from Puerto Rico, Cuba, and the Dominican Republic. The bracero program allowed Mexicans to work on American farms. After passage of the Immigration and Nationality Act Amendments in 1965, immigration from Latin America surged.

Following the lead of the civil rights movement, Latinos began fighting for their rights. The most influential Latino activist was Cesar Chavez, who formed the United Farm Workers (UFW). This union implemented a strike and boycott of grapes that secured safer working conditions for **migrant farmworkers**. These workers were often exploited as they moved from farm to farm to pick fruits and vegetables. A broader movement known as the **Chicano movement** worked to raise consciousness, reduce poverty and discrimination, and attain political power for Latinos.

Native Americans formed their own protest groups. One group took over the island of Alcatraz and claimed it for the Sioux. Another group, the American Indian Movement (AIM), was founded in 1968 to ease poverty and help secure legal rights and self-government for Native Americans. In February 1973, AIM took over Wounded Knee, South Dakota, to protest living conditions on reservations. That protest led to the deaths of two AIM members. Laws helping Native Americans were passed in the 1970s, including the Indian Self-Determination Act of 1975, which granted tribes greater control over resources on reservations.

The consumer rights movement started after Ralph Nader published *Unsafe at Any Speed*, a book that investigated the link between flawed car design and deaths in automobile accidents. The book prompted Congress to pass laws to improve automobile safety. Americans with disabilities, due in part to activism by Korean and Vietnam War veterans, also secured additional rights. Several laws were passed in the 1970s guaranteeing equal access to education for those with disabilities.

Lesson Vocabulary

migrant farmworkers   people who travel from farm to farm to pick fruits and vegetables

Chicano movement   movement to promote Mexican American social and political issues and culture

Name _____ Class _____ Date _____

TOPIC 18 LESSON 4

Lesson Summary
THE ENVIRONMENTAL MOVEMENT

MODIFIED CORNELL NOTES

Published in 1962, Rachel Carson's *Silent Spring* inspired much environmental activism. The book describes the deadly impact that pesticides were having on birds and other animals. Carson argued that humans were drastically altering the environment and had a responsibility to protect it. Protests sparked by the book eventually compelled Congress to restrict use of the pesticide DDT.

Other environmental concerns included toxic waste such as coal smog—poisonous **byproducts** of human activity. One response to environmental concerns was Earth Day. Close to 20 million Americans took part in the first Earth Day, held on April 22, 1970, and it has since become an annual event.

Public outcry over environmental issues convinced President Nixon to support environmental reforms. Under his leadership, Congress created the Environmental Protection Agency (EPA) in 1970 to protect "the entire ecological chain." The EPA worked to clean up and protect the environment and sought to limit or eliminate pollutants that posed a risk to the public's health. Nixon also signed a number of environmental laws. The Clean Air Act (1970) combated air pollution by limiting the **emissions** from factories and automobiles. The Clean Water Act (1973) reduced water pollution by industry and agriculture. The Endangered Species Act (1973) helped to protect endangered plants and animals.

In the late 1970s, several crises reinforced the public's environmental concern. Toxic waste in the ground was blamed for high rates of birth defects and cancer in Love Canal, New York. Later, a nuclear reactor at Three Mile Island in Pennsylvania malfunctioned and the core began to melt.

While these events solidified some people's support for environmental regulation, other people questioned and opposed the government's actions. Conservatives complained that regulation took away individuals' property rights. Others argued that private property owners, rather than the government, should protect the environment. Industry leaders worried that too much environmental regulation would harm business.

Lesson Vocabulary

byproduct additional material created during manufacturing or industrial production of a primary product

emission the act or instance of discharging a substance

Copyright © by Pearson Education, Inc., or its affiliates. All Rights Reserved.

Name _____ Class _____ Date _____

Topic 18, Lesson 5 — Lesson Summary: THE TWO SIDES OF THE NIXON PRESIDENCY

MODIFIED CORNELL NOTES

During his years as President, Richard Nixon fundamentally reshaped the way the United States approached the world. His leading adviser on national security and international affairs, Henry Kissinger, helped him.

In foreign affairs, Nixon and Kissinger shared the idea of **realpolitik**, a German word meaning "real politics." According to this idea, a nation's political goals around the world should be defined by what is good for the nation instead of by abstract ideologies.

In 1972, Nixon traveled to China and met with Premier Zhou Enlai and Chairman Mao Zedong. The visit was a historic first step toward normalizing relations between the two countries.

Nixon's trip to China was met by an immediate reaction from the Soviet Union. Soviet leader Leonid Brezhnev invited the President to visit Moscow, where they signed the first Strategic Arms Limitation Treaty. This agreement froze the deployment of intercontinental ballistic missiles and placed limits on antiballistic missiles. The treaty was a first step toward limiting the arms race.

The United States and Soviet Union now implemented a new policy called **détente** to replace the prior foreign policy, which was based on suspicion and distrust. Détente eased tensions between the two nations.

In 1968, Richard Nixon narrowly defeated Democrat Hubert Humphrey to win the presidency. During the campaign, Nixon claimed to represent the **silent majority**, the working men and women who made up middle America. He believed that they were tired of "big" government.

(Continues on the next page.)

Lesson Vocabulary

realpolitik a foreign policy based on concrete national interests instead of abstract ideologies; promoted by Henry Kissinger during the Nixon administration

détente flexible diplomacy adopted by President Richard Nixon to ease tensions between the United States, the Soviet Union, and the People's Republic of China

silent majority phrase introduced by President Richard Nixon to refer to a significant number of Americans who supported his policies but chose to not express their views

Name _____ Class _____ Date _____

TOPIC 18 LESSON 5

Lesson Summary
THE TWO SIDES OF THE NIXON PRESIDENCY (continued)

MODIFIED CORNELL NOTES

Nixon's presidency was plagued by a combination of recession and inflation that came to be known as **stagflation**. When the Organization of Petroleum Exporting Countries (OPEC) placed an oil embargo on Israel's allies, oil prices skyrocketed.

Nixon set out to expand his base of support. His **southern strategy** targeted southern whites, who had traditionally voted for Democrats.

In June 1972, burglars broke into the Democratic Party headquarters at the Watergate complex in Washington. After their conviction, one of them charged that administration officials had been involved. Nixon denied any wrongdoing in what came to be known as the Watergate scandal.

He claimed **executive privilege**, which is the principle that the President has the right to keep certain information confidential. However, the Supreme Court ordered Nixon to turn over the tapes. These tapes provided evidence of Nixon's involvement in the coverup. In order to avoid impeachment and conviction, Nixon resigned in August 1974.

Lesson Vocabulary

stagflation   term for the economic condition created in the late 1960s and 1970s by high inflation combined with stagnant economic growth and high unemployment

southern strategy   tactic of the Republican Party to win presidential elections by securing the electoral votes of southern states

executive privilege   principle that the President has the right to keep private certain communications between himself and other members of the executive branch

Copyright © by Pearson Education, Inc., or its affiliates. All Rights Reserved.

Name _____ Class _____ Date _____

Topic 18 Lesson 6

Lesson Summary
FORD AND CARTER STRUGGLE

MODIFIED CORNELL NOTES

Gerald Ford had a long record of public service. When he became President after Nixon's resignation, he had the support of Democrats as well as Republicans. However, he lost support when he announced that he had **pardoned**, or officially forgiven, Nixon for any crimes he might have committed as President.

Relations with the Soviet Union were central to U.S. foreign policy during the Ford and Carter administrations. President Gerald Ford and Soviet leader Leonid Brezhnev met twice and endorsed the Helsinki Accords. In this document, the nations of Europe expressed their support of **human rights**. However, Ford chose to put arms control ahead of human rights. The United States continued disarmament talks with the Soviets.

Former Georgia governor Jimmy Carter won the presidency in the 1976 election. A day after his inauguration, he granted **amnesty** to Americans who had evaded the draft, in the hope of moving the nation beyond the Vietnam War. Severe inflation continued, fueled by the ongoing energy crisis.

Early in his presidency, Jimmy Carter announced that his foreign policy would be guided by a concern for human rights. He tried to use his foreign policy to end acts of political repression, such as torture. Carter also worked to achieve détente, and in 1979, he signed the SALT II treaty to limit nuclear arms production. However, relations between the two superpowers took a frosty turn after the Soviet Union invaded Afghanistan in December 1979. Carter responded by imposing **sanctions** on the Soviets, including a boycott of the 1980 Summer Olympic Games in Moscow. Carter also hoped to change the way the United States dealt with the **developing world**. His emphasis on human rights led him to alter the U.S. relationship with a number of dictators.

(Continues on the next page.)

Lesson Vocabulary

pardoned   official forgiveness of a crime and its punishment

human rights   basic rights held by every human being, including religious freedom, education, and equality

amnesty   general pardon for certain crimes

sanctions   penalties intended to make people obey laws and rules, especially measures taken to force a country to obey international law

developing world   countries that are less economically advanced than developed countries such as the United States and those of Western Europe

TOPIC 18 LESSON 6

Lesson Summary
FORD AND CARTER STRUGGLE (continued)

MODIFIED CORNELL NOTES

Carter's greatest foreign policy success and setback were both in the Middle East. Egypt and Israel had been enemies since Israel's founding in 1948. In 1977, Carter invited the leaders of the two nations to the presidential retreat. The result was the Camp David Accords, which led to a peace treaty in which Egypt recognized Israel.

The 1970s also witnessed a resurgence of fundamental Christianity. **Televangelists** such as Jerry Falwell preached to millions on television. Religious conservatives opposed many of the social changes that begun in the 1960s and had gone mainstream in the 1970s. They began to form alliances with other conservatives to forge a new political majority.

Lesson Vocabulary

televangelists   ministers who use the television to preach

Name _____ Class _____ Date _____

TOPIC 18: Review Questions
AN ERA OF CHANGE

Answer the questions below using the information in the Lesson Summaries on the previous pages.

Lesson 1: The Counterculture of the 1960s

1. **Identify Main Ideas** How did social and political events help shape the counterculture?

2. What district in San Francisco was at the center of the counterculture?

Lesson 2: The Women's Rights Movement

3. **Cause and Effect** What inspired the second wave of feminism?

4. **Cause and Effect** What causes did the National Organization for Women work toward? Did its efforts succeed or fail?

Lesson 3: Expanding the Push for Equality

5. What organization did Cesar Chavez help organize?

6. **Compare and Contrast** Compare and contrast the goals of the United Farm Workers and the Chicano Movement.

Lesson 4: The Environmental Movement

7. What agency works to limit or eliminate pollution?

8. **Recognize Sequence** Which two events preceded President Nixon's environmental reforms?

Name _____ Class _____ Date _____

TOPIC 18 — Review Questions
AN ERA OF CHANGE (continued)

Lesson 5: The Two Sides of the Nixon Presidency

9. Identify Main Ideas How did Nixon improve relations between the United States and China, as well as the United States and the Soviet Union?

_____
_____

10. Why did President Nixon resign as president in 1974?

_____
_____

Lesson 6: Ford and Carter Struggle

11. What did President Ford prioritize over human rights?

_____
_____

12. What was President Carter's guiding principle for his foreign policy?

_____
_____

Name _____ Class _____ Date _____

TOPIC 19

Note Taking Study Guide

AMERICA IN THE 1980s AND 1990s

Focus Question: What were the major domestic and foreign policy issues during the 1980s and 1990s?

As you read, note specific examples of domestic and foreign policies implemented by Presidents Reagan, Bush, and Clinton.

I. Ronald Reagan

    A. Domestic _____

        1. _____

        2. _____

    B. Foreign Policy _____

        1. _____

        2. _____

II. _____

    A. Domestic _____

    B. Foreign Policy _____

        1. _____

        2. _____

III. _____

    A. Domestic _____

        1. _____

        2. _____

    B. Foreign Policy _____

        1. _____

        2. _____

Name _____ Class _____ Date _____

TOPIC 19 LESSON 1

Lesson Summary
THE CONSERVATIVE MOVEMENT SURGES

MODIFIED CORNELL NOTES

The two major political parties in the late twentieth century were the Democrats, many of whom were "liberals," and the Republicans, often labeled "conservatives." **Liberals** believed that the federal government should play an active role in improving the lives of all Americans. They supported social programs and government regulation of industry, and favored cooperation with international organizations such as the United Nations.

Conservatives believed that the free market, private organizations, and individuals, instead of the government, should care for the needy. They opposed big government, favored tax cuts, and supported a strong military.

Many things contributed to the conservative movement known as the New Right, which grew rapidly during the 1960s and 1970s. The Vietnam War and urban riots of the 1960s divided the country. The counterculture had alienated many Americans. Watergate, the oil crises of the 1970s, and the Iran hostage crisis further weakened the public's faith in the federal government. When the economy stagnated, conservative beliefs became more attractive.

Conservatives blamed liberal policies for the economic problems of the late 1970s. They believed that the government taxed too heavily and spent too much money on the wrong programs. They complained about **unfunded mandates**, programs required but not paid for by the federal government.

In 1979, Reverend Jerry Falwell founded the Moral Majority, a political organization based on religious beliefs. Its supporters worried about the decline of the traditional family. They were also concerned that the new freedoms brought by the counterculture would lead to the degeneration of modern youth.

The conservative movement swept the Republican presidential candidate, former actor and two-term California governor Ronald Reagan, to victory over Democratic incumbent Jimmy Carter in the 1980 election. Reagan's conservative beliefs, charm, and optimism convinced Americans that he would usher in a new era of prosperity and patriotism.

Lesson Vocabulary

liberals   people who tend to support government intervention to help the needy and favors laws protecting the rights of women and minorities

conservatives   people who tend to support limited government involvement in the economy, community help for the needy, and traditional values

unfunded mandates   program or action required but not paid for by the federal government

Copyright © by Pearson Education, Inc., or its affiliates. All Rights Reserved.

Name _____ Class _____ Date _____

Topic 19 Lesson 2: Lesson Summary — THE REAGAN ERA

MODIFIED CORNELL NOTES

President Reagan's economic policies, or "Reaganomics," were based on the theory of **supply-side economics**, which assumes that reducing taxes gives more people more incentive to work and more money to spend, causing the economy to grow. The government would then collect more tax dollars without raising taxes. Congress passed the Economic Recovery Act of 1981, which reduced taxes by 25 percent over three years.

Reagan called for **deregulation**, or the removal of government control over industries, including airline and telecommunications industries. He also appointed conservative judges to federal courts.

The economy experienced a severe recession from 1980 through 1982 but rebounded in 1983. Inflation fell and the Gross National Product increased. Still, the number of poor increased and the richest grew even richer. Reagan increased defense spending but failed to win cuts in other areas of the budget, leading to a **budget deficit**, a shortfall between money spent and money collected by the government. The **national debt**, the amount of money the government owes to owners of government bonds, also rose. Deficit problems worsened when the government had to bail out depositors of the nearly one thousand Savings and Loan banks that failed in the Savings and Loan (S&L) crisis of 1989.

Reagan faced other problems. American students were scoring lower on standardized tests, prompting conservatives to further lobby for **vouchers**, or government checks that could be used by parents to pay tuition at private schools. The nation also faced a new disease—Acquired Immunodeficiency Syndrome (AIDS). By the end of the 1980s, AIDS was the biggest killer of men between the ages of 20 and 40.

Despite these problems, Reagan remained popular and was overwhelmingly reelected in 1984. However, his momentum did not lead to a triumph for conservatives in Congress. Democrats retained control of the House of Representatives.

Lesson Vocabulary

supply-side economics   economic theory which says that reducing tax rates stimulates economic growth

deregulation   reduction or removal of government controls over an industry, based on the belief that more freedom leads to greater success and profitability

budget deficit   shortfall between the amount of money spent and the amount of money taken in by the federal government

national debt   total amount of money that the federal government owes to the holders of government bonds

voucher   certificate or other document that can be used in place of money

Name _____ Class _____ Date _____

TOPIC 19 LESSON 3
Lesson Summary
THE COLD WAR ENDS

MODIFIED CORNELL NOTES

Under President Reagan, the United States worked to weaken communism and the Soviet Union by committing to the largest peacetime military buildup in its history. Reagan believed that the Soviet Union would be unable to match U.S. defense spending. Reagan also proposed the Strategic Defense Initiative (SDI), which would use lasers to destroy missiles aimed at the United States. Furthermore, Reagan supported anticommunist rebellions worldwide, including the Contras, anticommunist counterrevolutionaries in Nicaragua.

Mikhail Gorbachev, who became the leader of the Soviet Union in 1985, initiated reforms to move the country away from a state-controlled economy. He pursued the policies of *glasnost*, meaning a new openness, and *perestroika*, reforming the Soviet system. As Reagan predicted, Gorbachev realized that the Soviet Union could not match the U.S. military buildup. Relations between the two nations improved. Both eventually signed a nuclear arms pact and began negotiating for a reduction of nuclear weapons.

The Cold War came to an end. The Berlin Wall tumbled in November 1989. From 1989 through 1991, communists lost power in Poland, Hungary, Czechoslovakia, Bulgaria, Romania, Albania, and Yugoslavia. And the Soviet Union split into 15 independent republics when it collapsed in 1991.

In the Middle East, 241 United States Marines stationed in Lebanon were killed by a truck bomb. The United States repeatedly clashed with Libya, whose leader, Muammar al-Qaddafi, supported terrorist groups. One breakthrough in Middle East affairs, minutes into Reagan's presidency, was the release of all 52 American hostages held by Iran. However, Reagan's second term was tarnished by the Iran-Contra affair. In 1985, the United States sold weapons to Iran in exchange for Iran's promise to pressure Lebanese terrorists to release American hostages, contradicting the administration's policy of refusing to negotiate with terrorists. Money from this sale was then used to fund Contras in Nicaragua, despite a congressional ban on such funding. Ultimately, several top officials were convicted of charges stemming from the scandal.

Lesson Vocabulary

glasnost Russian term for "new openness," a policy in the Soviet Union in the 1980s calling for open discussion of national problems

perestroika policy in the Soviet Union in the late 1980s calling for restructuring of the stagnant Soviet economy

Name _____ Class _____ Date _____

Topic 19 Lesson 4: Lesson Summary
A NEW ERA IN FOREIGN POLICY

MODIFIED CORNELL NOTES

Under President George H.W. Bush, the United States took a leading role in world affairs. Bush continued the war on drugs, and in December 1989, U.S. troops invaded Panama and arrested its dictator, Manuel Noriega. Noriega was convicted of drug trafficking and sentenced to 40 years in an American prison.

Iraq's invasion of Kuwait in August 1990 was one of Bush's greatest foreign policy challenges. Saddam Hussein, Iraq's dictator, sought to control Kuwait's rich oil deposits and increase his power in the region.

President Bush made it clear that he would not tolerate Iraq's aggression against its neighbor. He worked to build an international coalition and backed a United Nations resolution demanding that Iraqi troops withdraw. Hussein did not comply. Under the name Operation Desert Storm, American, British, French, Egyptian, and Saudi coalition forces attacked Iraqi troops on January 16, 1991.

Twelve years after the Reagan Revolution, Americans were ready for a change in the White House. The Democrats nominated William Jefferson Clinton, governor of Arkansas, to run against President Bush in the 1992 election. Texas billionaire H. Ross Perot ran as an independent. Clinton carried the election, and Democrats retained control of both houses of Congress.

On the political scene, many Americans opposed military involvement in foreign affairs, but Clinton found it necessary to intervene in conflicts in Somalia and Haiti. When civil war broke out in the former Yugoslav republic of Bosnia, Bosnian Serbs attacked and murdered Muslims and Croats. This state-sanctioned mass murder became known as **ethnic cleansing**. In 1995, Clinton asked NATO to bomb Serbian strongholds. This intervention brought about a cease-fire, but violence flared in another former Yugoslavian republic. NATO troops, including U.S. troops, responded again.

The ongoing conflict between Israelis and Palestinians escalated in the 1990s. Clinton led negotiations that produced a short-lived agreement between Israeli and Palestinian leaders. That involvement in the Middle East made the United States a target of a terrorist group called al Qaeda. The group launched several attacks on U.S. targets at home and abroad.

Lesson Vocabulary

ethnic cleansing systematic effort to purge a society of an ethnic group through murder or deportation

TOPIC 19 LESSON 5

Lesson Summary
CLINTON AND THE 1990S

MODIFIED CORNELL NOTES

Early in his presidency, Clinton focused on domestic issues. He signed the Family Medical Leave Act, which guaranteed most full-time employees unpaid leave each year for personal or family medical reasons. Clinton also oversaw passage of the Brady Bill, which placed a five-day waiting period on sales of handguns. Another important issue for Clinton was healthcare reform. Clinton's wife, Hillary, led a task force to investigate ways to guarantee healthcare for all Americans. The committee's proposal never won congressional support and was ultimately dropped.

In the 1994 midterm election, Georgia congressman Newt Gingrich led the opposition to Clinton. He galvanized Republicans around his Contract With America, a plan that attacked big government and emphasized patriotism and traditional values. Winning the votes of Americans who felt the federal government was too big, too wasteful, and too liberal, Republicans captured the House, the Senate, and most state governorships.

President Clinton had dodged scandals from his first day in office. One concerned investments the Clintons had made. Special prosecutor Kenneth Starr investigated the case for seven years but failed to uncover evidence of the Clintons' guilt. In the process, however, Starr investigated the President's relationship with a White House intern. When Clinton admitted he had lied about his affair with the intern under oath, Starr recommended **impeachment** proceedings. The House of Representatives impeached Clinton on the charges of perjury and obstruction of justice. Clinton was tried and acquitted by the Senate in February 1999.

The rapid pace of technological change in the twentieth century touched every aspect of modern life. One of the most important innovations was the computer. The first modern computer was developed in 1946 and filled an entire basement. As technology improved, small computers called personal computers were introduced. By the 1980s, **personal computers** were transforming American business and industry. They also changed medical science and helped create a new field called **biotechnology**, in which technology is used to solve problems affecting living organisms.

(Continues on the next page.)

Lesson Vocabulary

impeachment accusation against a public official of wrongdoing in office

personal computer small computer intended for individual use

biotechnology application of technology to solve problems affecting living organisms

Name _____ Class _____ Date _____

TOPIC 19 LESSON 5

Lesson Summary
CLINTON AND THE 1990S (continued)

MODIFIED CORNELL NOTES

The late twentieth century ushered in the "information age." **Satellites** orbiting Earth increased the speed of global communications. Cellular telephones using satellite technology enabled people to communicate away from their homes. By the 1990s, the Internet made communication and access to information almost instantaneous, which in turn profoundly altered commerce, education, research, and entertainment.

Lesson Vocabulary

satellite   mechanical device that orbits Earth, receiving and sending communication signals or transmitting scientific data

Copyright © by Pearson Education, Inc., or its affiliates. All Rights Reserved.

Name _____ Class _____ Date _____

TOPIC 19 — Review Questions
AMERICA IN THE 1980s AND 1990s

Answer the questions below using the information in the Lesson Summaries on the previous pages.

Lesson 1: The Conservative Movement Surges

1. Summarize Describe the differences between the liberal and conservative viewpoints of government.

2. What events contributed to the rise of conservatism?

Lesson 2: The Reagan Era

3. Identify Main Ideas Describe the central idea of Reagan's economic policies.

4. What occurred in the economy during the early 1980s?

Lesson 3: The Cold War Ends

5. Sequence Describe Mikhail Gorbachev's policies that brought reform to the Soviet Union prior to the collapse of communism.

6. Why did the Iran-Contra affair tarnish President Reagan's presidency?

Lesson 4: A New Era in Foreign Policy

7. Summarize Summarize President Bush's approach to Iraq's aggression toward Kuwait?

8. Why did President Clinton ask NATO to bomb Serbian strongholds?

Name _____ Class _____ Date _____

TOPIC 19: Review Questions
AMERICA IN THE 1980s AND 1990s (continued)

Lesson 5: Clinton and the 1990s

9. **Summarize** Summarize the difficulties President Clinton faced during his two terms in office.
_____
_____

10. What transformed American business and industry in the 1980s?
_____
_____

Name _____ Class _____ Date _____

TOPIC 20
Note Taking Study Guide
AMERICA IN THE TWENTY-FIRST CENTURY

Focus Question: How have modern-day U.S presidents handled domestic and foreign issues?

As you read, take notes about the domestic and foreign policy issues faced by modern-day U.S. presidents in the chart below. Note the main challenge, or problem, each U.S. president faced and how he attempted to solve the problem.

Problems	Solutions
•	•
•	•
•	•

Copyright © by Pearson Education, Inc., or its affiliates. All Rights Reserved.

187

Name _____ Class _____ Date _____

Topic 20 Lesson 1
Lesson Summary
AMERICA AND THE WORLD ECONOMY

MODIFIED CORNELL NOTES

In the 1990s, the United States was the world's sole superpower, wielding influence over economic and political events worldwide. Among the issues influenced by the United States was free trade. The European Union (EU), which coordinates monetary and economic policies among European nations, is an example of a free trade bloc. When the EU threatened U.S. economic leadership, the United States joined with Canada and Mexico to pass the North American Free Trade Agreement (NAFTA). NAFTA created a free trade zone in North America.

Clinton supported NAFTA and other free trade agreements, although many Democrats didn't. In 1994, he signed the revision to the General Agreement on Tariffs and Trade (GATT) aimed at reducing tariffs worldwide. In 1995, he signed the accords of the World Trade Organization (WTO), which replaced GATT and had greater authority to negotiate agreements and settle disputes.

Technological changes influenced how and where people worked. Fewer Americans worked in factories or on farms. Instead, they provided services. Satellites and computers increased **globalization**, the process by which national economies, politics, cultures, and societies become integrated with those of other nations around the world. A **multinational corporation** might have its financial headquarters in one country and manufacturing plants in several other countries. It might get raw materials from many different places and sell its products to a worldwide market.

Some economists say that the United States now has a **service economy**. Jobs in the service sector vary widely, from some of the highest paying, such as lawyers, to some of the lowest paying, such as fast-food workers. With the rise of the service economy and the decline of industries such as mining and manufacturing, the political power of labor unions has decreased and the average wages of workers have fallen.

Lesson Vocabulary

globalization   process by which national economies, politics, cultures, and societies mix with those of other nations around the world

multinational corporation   company that produces and sells their goods and services all over the world

service economy   economic system focused on the buying and selling of services

Name _____ Class _____ Date _____

TOPIC 20 LESSON 2

Lesson Summary
THE GEORGE W. BUSH PRESIDENCY

MODIFIED CORNELL NOTES

In the 2000 presidential election, Democrat Al Gore, Jr., ran against Republican George W. Bush. The results of the election were disputed. Democrats demanded a recount in Florida, where the vote was very close. Republicans sued to prevent the recount. The Supreme Court ended the recount and Bush won.

President Bush's domestic agenda focused on the economy and education. In 2002, Congress passed the No Child Left Behind Act. This penalized schools that did not reach federal performance standards and also called for improving teacher quality. He also promised to reform Social Security and Medicare. Although some progress was made with the Medicare Act of 2003, Democrats opposed Bush's reforms to Social Security.

On September 11, 2001, terrorists from the group al Qaeda launched a deadly attack against the United States. President Bush declared a war on terrorism. The Islamic fundamentalist Taliban government of Afghanistan refused to turn over al Qaeda leader Osama bin Laden. Bush then sent forces into Afghanistan. The Taliban was overthrown, but bin Laden escaped.

At home, improving national security became a priority. The Patriot Act gave law enforcement broader powers to monitor suspected terrorists. A new Cabinet-level Department of Homeland Security coordinated domestic security matters.

Bush turned his attention to Iraq. He asserted that Iraqi dictator Saddam Hussein had **weapons of mass destruction** and was a threat to U.S. security. In March 2003, American and British military forces invaded Iraq and soon toppled Saddam. However, violence erupted between ethnic groups and against American troops. In his second term, Bush's approval rating fell, and Democrats gained control of Congress. Voters became even more dissatisfied after a major financial crisis began in 2008.

Lesson Vocabulary

weapons of mass destruction nuclear, biological, and chemical weapons intended to kill or harm on a large scale

Name _____ Class _____ Date _____

TOPIC 20 LESSON 3 — Lesson Summary
THE BARACK OBAMA PRESIDENCY

MODIFIED CORNELL NOTES

In 2008, Democrat Barack Obama was elected as the first African American President. He ran against Republican nominee John McCain, a senator from Arizona. The two candidates had come from very different backgrounds. McCain was a former pilot and prisoner of war during the Vietnam War. He had served in Congress since 1982. Obama had served in the Illinois state legislature before being elected to the United States Senate. He had also been a community organizer in Chicago. The election drew a large voter turnout, with the majority of people citing the economy as their main concern.

Obama launched a stimulus package that pumped billions of dollars into the economy. Obama also ended the U.S. military mission in Iraq, focusing instead on the war in Afghanistan.

Obama also pursued healthcare reform. During his campaign, he pledged to provide affordable coverage for the more than 46 million Americans who had no health insurance. Finally, in March 2010, Congress passed the Affordable Care Act.

Less than two years into Obama's first term, the economy was still sluggish. Unemployment peaked at 10.2 percent in 2009. Although the economy had stabilized by the spring of 2010, unemployment remained high and growth was slow.

Some Americans, such as those in the Tea Party movement, felt that Obama's domestic programs were too costly and gave too much power to the federal government. Americans were also concerned about slow economic growth. In the 2010 elections, Republicans regained control of the House of Representatives.

The economy continued to remain a major concern for voters heading into the 2012 election. Obama's election campaign portrayed his opponent, Mitt Romney, as out of touch with ordinary people. This helped Obama win reelection.

Name _____ Class _____ Date _____

TOPIC 20 LESSON 4
Lesson Summary
AMERICANS LOOK TO THE FUTURE

MODIFIED CORNELL NOTES

As the twenty-first century dawned, American society looked very different than it had a hundred years before. The Immigration Act of 1990 had increased quotas by 40 percent and eased most restrictions. Since then, almost one million immigrants arrived in the United States each year. Most of the new immigrants were Latinos. They have had a profound social, cultural, and political impact. Asian countries make up the second-largest source of the new immigration.

Some people worry that immigrants take jobs and social services away from native-born Americans. They oppose **bilingual education**, in which students are taught in their native languages as well as in English. Proponents of immigration argue that immigrants contribute to the economy and help the nation maintain its population. Much of the debate concerns illegal immigrants. The Immigration and Control Act of 1986 aimed to stop the flow of illegal immigrants by penalizing businesses that hired them, but illegal immigrants still regularly cross U.S. borders.

American demographics have changed, as many people have moved from the Midwest and the Northeast to the Sunbelt. The American family changed as well. Divorces and single-parent households are now more common than they were just 40 years ago.

Affirmative action was created in the 1960s to help minorities and women overcome past discrimination by giving them preference in school admissions and job applications. Today, such programs are being challenged and in some cases, ended. Even so, women and African Americans continue to make social and political gains. More African Americans now earn middle-class incomes and hold college degrees. Women are protected against unfair treatment in the workplace. The 1994 Violence Against Women Act increased federal resources to apprehend and prosecute men guilty of violent acts against women.

As the baby boom generation reaches retirement, falling birthrates mean there may not be enough workers to pay for their Social Security benefits. President Bush proposed **privatizing** Social Security. This change would allow younger workers to invest some of their earnings in individual retirement accounts. Opponents defeated his proposal and the debate continues.

Lesson Vocabulary

bilingual education   system in which students are taught in their native languages as well as in English

affirmative action   policy that gives special consideration to women and minorities to make up for past discrimination

privatizing   to transfer from governmental ownership or control to private interests

Name _____ Class _____ Date _____

TOPIC 20: Review Questions
AMERICA IN THE TWENTY-FIRST CENTURY

Answer the questions below using the information in the Lesson Summaries on the previous pages.

Lesson 1: America and the World Economy

1. **Identify Main Ideas** What role did the United States play in global economics during the 1990s?

2. How did the rise of the service economy in the United States affect labor unions?

Lesson 2: The George W. Bush Presidency

3. Why was the outcome of the 2000 presidential election unusual?

4. **Recognize Sequence** Which event in Bush's presidency had the greatest influence on subsequent events? Explain.

Lesson 3: The Barack Obama Presidency

5. What was the main issue voters were concerned about in 2008?

6. **Recognize Effects** What effect did slow economic growth have on the 2010 election?

Lesson 4: Americans Look to the Future

7. How have American demographics changed in recent decades?

8. **Identify Supporting Details** What law increased resources to prosecute men guilty of violence against women?